OVERCOMING
NIGHT EATING
SYNDROME

A STEP-BY-STEP GUIDE TO
BREAKING THE CYCLE

KELLY C. ALLISON, PH.D.
ALBERT J. STUNKARD, MD
WITH SARA L. THIER

NEW HARBINGER PUBLICATIONS, INC.

Distributed in Canada by Raincoast Books

Copyright © 2004 by Kelly C. Allison, Albert J. Stunkard, and Sara L. Thier
New Harbinger Publications, Inc.
5674 Shattuck Avenue
Oakland, CA 94609

Cover design by Amy Shoup
Edited by Kayla Sussell
Text design by Tracy Marie Carlson

ISBN-10 1-57224-327-9
ISBN-13 978-1-57224-327-9

FSC
Mixed Sources
Product group from well-managed
forests and other controlled sources

Cert no. SW-COC-002283
www.fsc.org
© 1996 Forest Stewardship Council

New Harbinger Publications' website address: www.newharbinger.com

11   10   09

10   9   8   7   6   5   4

To my son, Tyler. You were with me and inspired me every step of the way.

—Kelly C. Allison

To Elana and Keith, as you start your life together.

—Albert J. Stunkard

To my parents, Paula and Sam, who always believe in me. I treasure your support and love.

—Sara L. Thier

Contents

PART I
What You Need to Know about Night Eating

Acknowledgments

This book is the fruit of many years of research. Those many years, dating back to the 1950s, were possible first and foremost, because of the patients suffering from night eating syndrome (NES) who were willing to share their stories. The research that led to this book was also made possible through the support of our wonderful colleagues.

The NES research team at the University of Pennsylvania's Weight and Eating Disorders Program has been instrumental in furthering our understanding of NES. Dr. John O'Reardon has provided guidance and ingenuity in his work with NES. Our research assistants, Nicole Martino, Heidi Toth, Heidi Marshall, and Dr. Pilar Cristancho put in many hours working with patients as well as reviewing data and keeping the nuts and bolts of the program running smoothly. Thanks go to sleep research experts Dr. David Dinges and Dr. Naomi Rogers for dedicating their energies toward describing sleep among people with NES. We also thank all of the students who have worked with us over the past few years; they brought energy and creativity to our work.

We would also like to thank our colleagues for their encouragement in our research efforts and in writing this book. Drs. Berkowitz, Faith, Foster, Sarwer, Wadden, and Womble are dedicated to the study and treatment of obesity. They are role models in the field and supportive through both their expertise and friendship. Thanks as well to Dr. Angie Makris and Dr. Jackie Kloss for providing feedback on nutrition and therapeutic methods for sleep, respectively.

Thank you to the editors from New Harbinger Publications who initiated the writing of this book. Editors Jueli Gastwirth and Melissa Kirk kept us on track during the writing process, and Kayla Sussell was very helpful in copyediting the manuscript.

We would also like to thank our families, who, as always, were there with their patience and acceptance of the extra hours devoted to writing this book.

Finally, special thanks to the many people we have met over the years who were kind enough to tell us about their experiences with NES to us so that, step-by-step, we can come to understand and treat this syndrome more effectively.

Introduction

If you suffer from Night Eating Syndrome (NES), you know that it is disruptive to your life and damaging to your health, but only recently have health providers and the public begun to recognize it as a serious problem needing treatment. Characterized by lack of appetite in the morning, overeating at night, and waking to eat throughout the night, NES has started receiving more publicity and, just as important, more funding for research to find better ways of treating this complex problem.

Remember you are not alone. About 9 percent of people seen in clinics for treatment of obesity are also suffering from NES. Although you do not have to be obese to suffer from NES, approximately a third or more of individuals who are extremely overweight, ranging from 27 to 42 percent, also have NES (Hsu, Betancourt, and Sullivan 1996; Rand, Macgregor, and Stunkard 1997). Both men and women are affected by NES, with men representing over 40 percent of all people with the syndrome. By reading this book and working through the exercises, you will learn about the different components of the syndrome and how each component has targeted treatments that can help to reduce your problems with NES.

Why We Wrote This Book

Our intention throughout this book is to offer you hope and help. We are well aware that some of the physicians you may visit might not even acknowledge your problem, so we feel that our book will fill an important gap in providing information and guiding you to take charge of your health, your weight, and your life.

Who We Are

Dr. Albert Stunkard. Of the three of us, Dr. Stunkard has the longest history of working with NES. In fact, in 1955 Dr. Stunkard and two of his colleagues were the first to identify and publish an article about NES (Stunkard, Grace, and Wolff 1955; Stunkard 1959). Though more than fifty years have passed since he first learned about night eating syndrome, his introduction to it was so dramatic that it has stayed with him to this day.

Dr. Stunkard recalls, "I was then a resident-in-training for psychiatry and I was treating Maxine, a sixteen-year-old high-school student who had been referred to the Psychiatry Clinic for obesity and for depression. At the time, obesity was widely viewed as an eating disorder, and psychotherapy was considered an appropriate treatment for it as well as for depression. Over a period of three months Maxine made considerable progress; she lost ten pounds and came out of her depression, smiling and full of life. At this point she reported a series of troubling interactions with her father, who had begun to sexualize their relationship. Then one evening she arrived at my office to tell me, mournfully, that her parents had told her that she could not continue therapy.

"Thoroughly disappointed with this outcome, I turned to a small group of fellow trainees who regularly met to discuss patients and problems and offer support to each other. While discussing Maxine, I turned on an audiotape to convey a feeling for her mood. All of a sudden, one of the trainees, an obese young woman, gasped for air, rose from the floor on which we had been sitting, and staggered out of the room. I followed her to find her in the middle of a panic attack. After she had recovered, she returned to the group and explained what had happened.

"To our questioning about what had disturbed her, she volunteered, 'I wasn't disturbed by the problems with the father, although they were really distressing. What bothered me was the way that girl talked about how she eats. She isn't hungry in the morning, all morning. Then at night, she can't seem to stop eating. Supper doesn't satisfy her and she just goes on and on. She even gets up out of bed to eat. That's how I eat, and I've never heard about anyone eating that way besides me in my whole life!'"

As Dr. Stunkard continued treating obese patients, this event stayed with him, and he began to encounter others with the same eating pattern. Over the years, he and his colleagues have learned more and more about this disorder and they are now in a position to offer guidance and hope to those of you who suffer from night eating syndrome and to your relatives and friends. This book is an effort to provide this guidance and this hope.

Dr. Kelly Allison. Dr. Allison is newer to the field of NES than is Dr. Stunkard. Currently, she directs the Night Eating Syndrome study at the University of Pennsylvania. Her interest in NES was aroused after hearing Dr. Stunkard describe its unusual eating, sleeping, and mood patterns. As a clinical psychologist, she knew the complexities involved in treating each of these disorders individually. The combination of these problems was certainly unique and presented a challenge she was eager to take on.

She said, "Not only did I want to know more about the syndrome itself, but also I wanted to meet and help those who live with it day to day. Having the opportunity to listen to the stories of the people suffering with NES allowed me to hear the frustration and even desperation in their voices. Working directly with these individuals has provided me greater insight into both the theoretical background and the reality of NES."

Dr. Allison, along with Dr. Stunkard and other dedicated researchers, continues to search for ways to help patients take control of NES and their lives.

Ms. Sara Thier. Sara Thier's career path has focused on educating and motivating patients to take a more active role in their own health care. She hopes that her experience with changing health care behavior will help to translate the work of Drs. Stunkard and Allison into steps and strategies that you can put into practice almost immediately.

We all wish you the best of luck as you work your way through the exercises in the book, and we are certain that the book will help guide you toward your goals for recovery.

Is This Book for You?

This book is for you if you suspect you may be affected by NES. This book is also for you if you are concerned about a family member or friend who may be affected by NES. Both women and men are affected, although probably about 60 percent of the sufferers are women (Allison et al., Working paper 2004). Night eating syndrome usually develops in people in their twenties or thirties, but for some it may begin earlier or later because of a strong familial, that is, genetic, component in their eating behaviors or in response to a stressful life situation. We hope that this book will provide you with insights into why you are having problems, what the causes of those problems are, and what possible solutions may be available to you.

In chapter 1, Beth's story offers you a typical experience of a night eater. Reading her story, you may notice some parallels to your own behavior. The Night Eating Questionnaire in this chapter will allow you to determine whether you may have NES. In chapter 2, we discuss the way that unusual eating habits play a key role in NES. Here, you will learn more about the eating patterns related to NES and how they differ from most people's eating habits. We also discuss whether there are actions you can take to change your eating patterns.

For night eaters, trying to fall asleep can be quite difficult. In chapter 3, you will learn how, as a night eater, your experiences with sleep differ from those of the typical person. We discuss circadian rhythms and we provide more knowledge about your sleep. In chapter 4, we consider the role of emotions in NES. Night eating can cause you to feel as if you are on an emotional roller coaster. How do your emotions feed into your NES? Chapter 5 asks, Do you really have night eating syndrome? Here you will learn how other eating, sleeping, and mood disorders are similar to NES, and how they differ from it.

How did you develop night eating? Chapter 6 helps you to examine your family history to learn how your genes may have played a role in your developing NES. Your body also produces hormones to help with various tasks. They can trigger both hunger and the need to sleep. In chapter 7, you will learn more about the role that hormones play in your life and how their imbalance can contribute to your troubles with night eating. Chapter 8 describes the four types of NES. Which of them can you relate to most? Can changing your thought patterns really change your behaviors? Try some of the activities and see.

Chapter 9 introduces the role that imagery, relaxation, and behavioral interventions can play when dealing with NES. Take a deep breath, relax, and learn how to counter NES with relaxation techniques. Most people need support when making changes in their lives, and modifying your night eating behaviors is no different. Chapter 10 will guide you in how to ask for support from family and friends, and how you, in turn, can support others who have NES.

Although there are very few medications for NES, in chapter 11 you can learn more about what other night eaters have tried and some promising developments for the future. Chapter 12 offers our final thoughts about NES and encouragement for the changes you hope to accomplish. The Resources section lists many Web sites that you may find helpful, and the References section provides all the information you need if you wish to study a particular topic in greater depth.

PART I

What You Need to Know about Night Eating

Chapters 1 through 5 will help you to determine whether you have night eating syndrome (NES) by exploring the eating, sleeping, and mood patterns associated with the syndrome. You will become acquainted with what it is really like to suffer with NES, and how NES differs from other problems that may have similar symptoms.

CHAPTER 1

Are You a
Night Eater?

When did you first become aware of night eating syndrome (NES)? If you have never heard it called this name before, that's okay. That's also true for most of the public and the majority of health care providers. It's been only recently that discussions of NES have appeared in a few magazines and on some Web sites. Although you and others with this condition may not have been able to label your eating habits as NES, the problems you face are very real and very challenging. For example, consider Beth's situation:

Beth is a forty-five-year-old mother of three who is worried about her eating habits. She says that during the day she doesn't eat much at all. But in the evening and late at night she finds herself eating most of her daily intake of food. She attributes this unusual eating pattern not only to caring for and worrying about her kids, but also to the fact that she is working two part-time jobs. She has a hard time falling asleep and wakes up in the middle of the night needing to eat in order to fall asleep again.

Beth believes that this pattern of night eating began ten years ago when her last child, Emily, was born with Down's syndrome. Since that time, Beth has experienced great stress in caring for her daughter. After Emily's birth, Beth was unable to lose the weight she had gained during pregnancy and she continued putting on more weight. She is approximately fifty-five pounds overweight and feels depressed about her inability to lose those extra pounds. The mental and physical stress of caring for her developmentally disabled daughter, along with her inability to control her night eating and her increasing weight, have left her feeling depressed and hopeless.

The Primary Signs of Night Eating Syndrome

Beth's situation is characteristic of someone with NES. There are five primary signs that characterize NES. These signs are discussed below:

- **Not feeling hungry in the morning:** If you have NES, most likely you will not have any appetite at all in the morning and will often go without food or even lack the desire to eat until lunchtime or the afternoon.

- **Overeating in the evening:** In contrast to a lack of appetite in the morning, if you have NES, you will feel very hungry in the evening and will overeat. Overeating with NES is different from binge eating in most cases. This difference is discussed in chapter 2.

- **Difficulty falling asleep:** If you have NES, you may find it hard to fall asleep; you may toss and turn for half an hour or longer. You may need to eat something just before you go to bed to fall asleep faster.

- **Waking at night and eating:** If you have NES, after falling asleep you may wake at least once during the night, and you'll find it necessary to eat before you're able to fall asleep again.

- **Feeling depressed:** In addition to your eating and sleeping problems, you may feel very sad or stressed. Whether these feelings are directly related to NES or caused by an external event, they influence your ability to control your NES.

Do you have night eating syndrome? To find out, take the following Night Eating Questionnaire.

Night Eating Questionnaire

Directions: Please circle one answer for each question.

1. How hungry are you usually in the morning?

  0 Very

  1 Moderately

  2 Somewhat

  3 A little

  4 Not at all

2. When do you usually eat for the first time?

  0 Before 9 A.M.

  1 9:01 to 12 P.M.

  2 12:01 to 3 P.M.

  3 3:01 to 6 P.M.

  4 6:01 P.M. or later

3. Do you have cravings or urges to eat snacks after supper, but before bedtime?

  0 Not at all

  1 A little

  2 Somewhat

  3 Very much so

  4 Extremely so

4. How much control do you have over your eating between supper and bedtime?

  0 Complete

  1 Very much

  2 Some

  3 A little

  4 None at all

5. How much of your daily food intake do you consume after suppertime?

0 0 percent (none)

1 1 to 25 percent (up to a quarter)

2 26 to 50 percent (about half)

3 51 to 75 percent (more than half)

4 76 to 100 percent (almost all)

6. Are you currently feeling blue or down in the dumps?

0 Not at all

1 A little

2 Somewhat

3 Very much so

4 Extremely so

7. When you're feeling blue, is your mood lower in the

0 Early morning

1 Late morning

2 Afternoon

3 Early evening

4 Late evening or nighttime

_____ Check here if your mood does not change during the day.

8. How often do you have trouble getting to sleep?

0 Never

1 Sometimes

2 About half the time

3 Usually

4 Always

9. **Other than to use the bathroom, how often do you get up at least once in the middle of the night?**

   0 Never

   1 Less than once a week

   2 About once a week

   3 More than once a week

   4 Every night

If you answered 0 on question 9, please stop here.

10. **Do you have cravings or urges to eat snacks when you wake up at night?**

    0 Not at all

    1 A little

    2 Somewhat

    3 Very much so

    4 Extremely so

11. **Do you need to eat in order to get back to sleep when you awake at night?**

    0 Not at all

    1 A little

    2 Somewhat

    3 Very much so

    4 Extremely so

12. **When you get up in the middle of the night, how often do you snack?**

    0 Never

    1 Sometimes

    2 About half the time

    3 Usually

    4 Always

If you answered 0 on question 12, please stop here.

13. When you snack in the middle of the night, how aware are you of your eating?

0 Not at all

1 A little

2 Somewhat

3 Very much so

4 Completely

14. How much control do you have over your nighttime eating?

0 Complete

1 Very much

2 Some

3 A little

4 None at all

Calculating your score: To calculate your score, simply add up the numbers you circled.

Interpreting your score: When interpreting your results, it is important to realize that not every night eater has all of the signs of NES. For example, some NES sufferers may not wake up in the middle of the night to eat, but they may still consume most of their food during the evening, before going to bed.

If you scored **over 30,** you probably are suffering from NES. We believe that you will benefit from reading each of the chapters thoroughly and practicing the suggested steps for conquering this condition.

If you scored **under 30,** you may not be a night eater in the clinical sense of the diagnosis. But look at your answers to assess which NES characteristics concern you and which chapters might be helpful to you.

Did you score higher on questions related to your eating patterns while you are awake? (Questions 1, 2, 3, 4, 5) Read chapters 2 and 8 to learn more about how to regulate your eating.

Did you score higher on questions related to depression? (Questions 6, 7) Read chapter 4 to learn more about mood disorders. Night eaters often feel worse in the evening, so if you checked that your mood does not change, don't add any points to your total.

Did you score higher on questions related to your sleeping patterns? (Questions 8, 9) Read chapters 3, 8, and 9 to learn more about how to improve your sleep. If you were instructed to stop at question 9, you don't get up during the night, and the remaining questions don't apply to you.

Did you score higher on questions related to your nighttime eating? (Questions 10, 11, 12) If you've made it past question 9, you probably are dealing with NES and would benefit from working through the whole book. If you stopped at question 12, you don't get up to eat when you wake at night. So questions 13 and 14 don't apply to you.

Did you score high on the questions related to your nighttime eating awareness and control? (Questions 13, 14) You are definitely dealing with issues related to NES. If you score low on 13, you may be suffering from *nocturnal sleep-related eating disorder* (NS-RED), which differs from NES in that you are essentially asleep and unaware of your eating. This is called a *parasomnia*, or sleep disorder. NS-RED may have different treatment options from NES, although research for NS-RED is still in its early stages. Read chapter 5 to learn more about NS-RED, as well as other sleep and eating disorders you might be experiencing.

Although signs and symptoms may vary from person to person, NES is not a condition to be overlooked or underestimated.

The Consequences of Night Eating

Like many people, you may blame your night eating on poor self-control, believing you should be able to manage your eating habits. One woman wrote, "Thank goodness I have discovered that this is a real disorder. I feel like a pig and somehow like a person with a dirty secret. I am embarrassed about my lack of self-control and angry that I am sabotaging my health and my weight-loss goals with this behavior."

Your doctor may also attribute the problem to bad habits and may not recognize NES as a condition that requires careful treatment. Yet, as you will learn in the chapters ahead, NES is not simply a bad habit. Neither is it just an eating disorder. It is also a sleep and mood disorder. Both biological and psychological factors play important roles in the development and persistence of this condition.

NES and Your Health

Overeating caused by NES can lead to weight gain and a variety of health conditions. Research has found that about 9 to 15 percent of those people seen in clinics for treatment of obesity are also suffering from NES (Stunkard, Berkowitz, Wadden, et al. 1996; Gluck, Geliebter, and Satov 2001). This percentage increases to 28 percent for those who are severely obese and who have been evaluated for surgical treatment for their obesity (Rand, Macgregor, and Stunkard 1997).

However, you may be one of the many night eaters who are not overweight. Approximately half of all overweight night eaters were of normal weight before they started night eating (Allison et al. Working paper 2004). Night eaters who begin or remain at a healthy weight may feel compelled to exercise or to restrict their calories during the day in their efforts to keep from gaining weight. These measures can be healthy for you, but don't overdo them. Obsessively maintaining preventive weight-gain behaviors also can take a toll on your mood, body image, and self-esteem over time.

Overweight and obesity themselves are serious conditions. Sixty-five percent of Americans are overweight; 30 percent are obese; and 5 percent are severely obese (Flegal et al. 2002). These numbers themselves are cause for concern, but the health conditions related to overweight and obesity pose even greater threats to your health and quality of life. Type II diabetes, high blood pressure, arthritis, heart disease, and asthma are just some of the serious conditions that may result from excess weight or become worse due to it.

As you can see, overweight and obesity are conditions to take seriously. They are diagnosed with the use of the body mass index (BMI), which tells you if you are normal weight, overweight, or obese. BMI is easy to calculate. If you wish to calculate your BMI, see the appendix to learn how to do it.

Medical Complications of NES Caused by Obesity

If you aren't already motivated to stop your night eating, knowing that it may be a pathway to obesity could provide an extra reason to try the strategies we recommend, that is, either cognitive and behavioral approaches and/or medications (see chapters 8 through 11). Gaining weight is probably the most direct medical implication of night eating, although acid reflux may also occur. The other conditions described below are often the result of excess weight gained by those who suffer from NES, so they represent secondary conditions of NES.

Acid reflux: More commonly known as heartburn, *acid reflux* occurs when the muscle that controls the opening between the esophagus and the stomach either does not close all the way or opens too often. Typically, this muscle opens to allow food to pass to the stomach or to belch up air from the stomach. However, for people with acid reflux, the muscle opens at other times, allowing stomach acid to rise into the esophagus, causing a burning sensation. Different types of foods are often linked to acid reflux, such as spicy foods, citrus fruits, tomatoes, or caffeine. Acid reflux can also be caused by obesity and is often experienced during pregnancy, since in both conditions there is more pressure placed on the stomach and esophagus, forcing the muscle to open and allowing the stomach acid to seep out.

There may also be a link between eating too quickly and acid reflux. Thus, eating quickly at night and returning to bed may cause a flare-up of acid reflux. If this condition becomes an almost daily occurrence, it can develop into *gastroesophageal reflux disease* (GERD). Gastroesophageal reflux disease is chronic heartburn that can have more serious side effects, ranging from chronic coughing to cancer of the esophagus. If you suffer from acid reflux, slow down your eating and change the foods you eat. Include more mild foods and less caffeine. This is good advice for night eaters, whether you have acid reflux or not. And, as always, consult your physician about possible treatments.

Type II diabetes: When the body is unable to use insulin properly, *type II diabetes* results. Insulin helps the body to process sugar for use as energy by the body's cells. If enough insulin is not available, or if its effectiveness is reduced, then sugar doesn't move readily from the bloodstream into the cells. One result is high levels of blood sugar. Over time, these high levels of blood sugar can lead to problems with your eyes, heart, kidneys, and nervous system. Obesity is considered to be a major cause of impaired insulin action.

Until recently, type II diabetes was considered primarily a disease of middle- and older-aged individuals (forty-five and older), and was known as "adult onset diabetes." However, the face of type II diabetes is changing. The increasing levels of over-weight and obesity in the United States, that have now reached 65 percent of the total population, have been accompanied by a 76 percent increase in type II diabetes in adults in the thirty- to forty-year-old category since 1990 (Flegal et al. 2002; Mokdad et al. 2001). The increase in obesity has affected younger and younger people, reaching down now to children, and it has been accompanied by the development of type II diabetes in children. Type II diabetes is no longer confined to an adult onset, and the endocrine clinics of children's hospitals are, for the first time, seeing large numbers of children with this disease (Goran, Ball, and Cruz 2003; Sinha et al. 2002).

There is no direct connection between NES and developing diabetes. However, the higher rates of NES in obese and morbidly obese patients, and the tendency for night eaters to put on weight, increases the likelihood that night eaters may already suffer from or will develop diabetes.

If you do have diabetes, your choice of foods and eating times becomes even more important. Since many cases of type II diabetes can be controlled with dietary and exercise changes, your erratic eating habits and bad food choices, for example, sugars and carbohydrates, can leave you at greater risk of developing devastating health complications from your diabetes. If you do not have diabetes, but have found that your night eating is causing you to gain weight, this is the time to nip it in the bud and control your night eating. This book is a good place to begin.

High blood pressure (hypertension): Blood pressure is the measure of the force of blood against the walls of your arteries. While pressure rises and falls naturally throughout the day, *high blood pressure* means that the force remains consistently elevated. This stress on the heart can lead to stroke, heart disease, and heart and kidney failure. There are no signs or symptoms of high blood pressure until it has already caused problems. How does this relate to overweight and obesity? Blood pressure rises as body weight increases. Although it is important for you to get your blood pressure checked regularly, if you are overweight or obese due to night eating syndrome, it is even more important. Even a modest weight loss of 10 percent can significantly reduce your blood pressure and lower your risk of further complications. If you currently weigh two hundred pounds, this translates into losing twenty pounds. If weight loss does not reduce your blood pressure to normal levels, be sure to ask your doctor about medications to treat it. The steps you take to conquer your night eating can also lead to a reduction in your blood pressure.

Osteoarthritis: Commonly called arthritis, *osteoarthritis* affects the joints, most often in the knees, hips, and lower back. Although overweight and obesity are not causes of arthritis, they contribute to the severity of the symptoms. If NES causes you to gain excess weight, that weight on already stressed joints causes increased pain and reduces mobility. Weight loss will not repair damage that has already occurred to joints, but the pain will be reduced and mobility will be increased.

Heart disease: Overweight or obesity resulting from NES can cause your overall risk for heart disease to increase. When combined with other health conditions, such as high blood pressure and diabetes, as well as unhealthy lifestyle risk factors like smoking, your probability of having heart disease will be even higher.

Asthma: If you suffer from asthma, you are aware when your airways tighten as a result of your exposure to a number of triggers, such as pet dander, exercise, secondhand smoke, or dust. As with arthritis, obesity may not be a cause of asthma, but excess weight caused by NES can create more pressure on already constricted airways leading to more frequent or more severe asthma attacks.

Excessive Daytime Sleepiness

If you suffer from NES, you may be like many others with the condition who have difficulty falling asleep, or even more trouble staying asleep. Some night eaters report waking up two or three times a night, and they find that only eating will allow them to fall back to sleep. This disruption in your sleeping pattern can lead to what is known as *excessive daytime sleepiness* (EDS). Excessive daytime sleepiness can interfere with your ability to concentrate, to perform everyday activities, and to focus on your tasks at work. This type of sleepiness differs from the feeling of being a little overtired or the fatigue you might feel if you are depressed. When you feel depressed, it may seem as if you have no energy to complete tasks or to engage in mentally challenging jobs, but you probably do not feel sleepy, as if you are about to fall asleep at any minute during the day.

Conversely, if you have EDS, you may drift off to sleep while sitting in a meeting, while watching television or a movie, or even while engaging in a conversation. The most serious aspect of EDS, however, occurs when you drive a car. Excessive daytime sleepiness is one of the most common causes of automobile accidents, ranking just behind driving while intoxicated. As you can see, living with the sleep patterns related to NES can contribute to EDS, which can be not only frustrating, but also dangerous.

Depression and Stress

Depression is common among night eaters, and some sufferers complain of a long-term struggle with feeling blue. Night eating also involves depression, which may be cause for concern. Stress is another problem. Life stress is associated with the onset of night eating in 75 percent of sufferers (Allison et al., Working paper 2004)—and it plays a role in the continuation of NES.

Have you experienced a particularly stressful situation in your life recently, such as the birth of a baby or the loss of your job? If so, these events may make your NES worse. Ironically, NES itself and your reaction to it also can perpetuate stress. You can think of night eating and depression, as well as night eating and stress, as vicious cycles. They are like a *Catch-22* situation. Breaking these cycles will help to release you from the night eating loop.

Beth's continuous stress caused by caring for her disabled child and working two jobs increases her night eating. The more this stress contributes to her awakenings and eating, the less sleep she gets at night and the more weight she gains. This leads to her feeling tired all the time, which in turn makes it more difficult to focus and to concentrate during her workday. The weight gain also makes her feel depressed about her appearance and increases her health concerns.

If Beth does not change a part of this pattern, the cycle will continue. To interrupt the unhealthy aspects of these areas in your life, we will help you figure out your patterns of eating, sleeping, and mood. When you have this information, you can start to challenge NES.

Getting Help from Others

For many people, NES is an embarrassing and secret disorder. Compared to other eating and sleeping disorders, very little attention has been focused on NES. As a result, the general public is often not aware of the problems that you are facing, and they may have little understanding of them. Thus, getting help from others may be difficult, but we encourage you to talk to others, including those we've listed below.

Your Heath Care Professionals and NES

Although we know that not many people are informed about NES yet, it seems particularly disturbing that even the health care providers you regularly see may not know much about the disorder. It is not uncommon for people with NES to have horror stories of visits to professionals. Even when they are politely received, they may get only a chuckle and a wag of the finger "to stop this eating at night." It is rare for the health care professional to make a substantial effort to sit down with the night eater and to figure out a treatment plan. You may have had similar frustrating experiences of your own. These experiences, in turn, foster your feelings of embarrassment and guilt.

Don't let experiences like this discourage you. Look for a health care provider who is sensitive to your needs. Work with a doctor or clinic that specializes in overweight and obesity. They are usually more up to date on conditions such as NES. Be sure to share the information you gather from this book and other sources about NES with your health care provider and make your concerns known to him or her. Although they may not be fully informed about the condition, good providers will take the time to learn about your specific problems in order to provide better care. Don't let your health care provider dismiss your concerns or your problems. If you are not receiving the care you deserve, find another provider who is more responsive to your needs.

In addition to seeking a concerned health care professional for help with your night eating, you may also want to find a professional to help you work through its emotional aspects. Seeing a psychiatrist, psychologist, or therapist can be very helpful in dealing with the various problems and situations that may be contributing to your stress and depression. In chapter 10, we will discuss how to decide which professional may best fit your needs.

Your Family or Roommates and NES

You not only may be embarrassed to tell your health care provider about your NES, you also may not feel comfortable talking about it with your friends and family. Your getting up at night may be interfering with the sleep of your bed partner or others in your home. Roommates and family members may notice that their favorite foods are disappearing at night. They may feel a mix of emotions about your behaviors: concern, frustration, even anger. You may then feel even guiltier and more anxious about your night eating and your inability to stop it. As you read further, we hope that you will find some ways to talk to your family and roommates about your struggles and ultimately to gain control over your night eating. See chapter 10 for help in how to go about discussing NES with your family and other housemates.

Your Friends and NES

Because your NES affects many aspects of your well-being, such as the quality of sleep, your weight, and your emotional life, you may want to turn to friends for understanding and support. Like health care professionals, your friends may not know much about NES, and they may have a hard time understanding and accepting the distress you feel. They may not empathize with the out-of-control feeling that you experience each night.

Have you told any of your friends? If you have, think about their reactions. Were they supportive, understanding? If you haven't told your friends, is it because you are afraid they will have a negative reaction or brush off your concerns as insignificant? By opening up to your friends, you may be surprised to learn that they know someone else with NES or that they even may have problems with night eating themselves. These issues are discussed in greater depth in chapter 10.

Starting a Journal and Dealing with Family and Roommates

How are you handling your family's or roommates' responses? Do you talk with them about their concerns about you? Have you tried any strategies to stay away from their food? Take a moment to think about what you have tried up to this point, and write about your efforts in a blank notebook or journal. While you are reading this book and working with the exercises, you should record your work in a journal. At first, it may seem like a burden to write down your thoughts, but you will come to see how helpful it can be to read back those thoughts a few days or weeks after you record them. Throughout this book we will ask you to write in your notebook or journal. Give it a try. Here are some examples to start you off. Note that there are no wrong answers.

What You Can Say to Your Family or Roommates

1. I need your help; I feel like I can't control my eating at night.

2. I'm sorry I ate your cookies last night. I really try not to eat them, but when I'm up at night, I can't seem to control what I eat.

3. Did you hear me get up last night? I'm sorry if I woke you up. Did you say anything to try to stop me from eating?

How You Can Stop Eating Your Forbidden Foods or Your Family or Roommates' Foods

1. Stop buying foods that are tempting to you or foods that you really like to eat at night.

2. Ask your roommates or children to keep their favorite foods in their rooms or someplace you won't go to at night.

3. Set out foods that you allow yourself to eat before you go to bed, so that they are within easy reach. Store more

tempting foods in more out-of-the-way places, like the basement, garage, or car.

These approaches are explored in further depth in part III. As you come to understand NES more thoroughly, you will be better equipped to educate others about your struggles and to seek and find the support that you need. The chapters to come will supply you with more information about NES, especially the new scientific discoveries. These discoveries will provide you with easy-to-implement steps that will aid you in your journey toward healthier eating and sleeping routines.

This Chapter's Goals

- Take the Night Eating Questionnaire. How many of the symptoms of night eating do you have?

- Start thinking about how your night eating affects your health and your relationships.

- Keep an open mind about what you are about to read.

- Get a blank journal so you can complete the exercises to come.

CHAPTER 2

Eating Patterns:
Food for Thought

A normal twenty-four-hour day for a night eater looks drastically different from the day of someone with no eating disorder. This chapter will compare and contrast the typical person's eating habits with the habits that you, with NES, will probably find more familiar. Learning to use some common tools, such as food diaries and meal planning, will give you better grasp of your eating patterns. Meal plans and food diaries provide the beginning steps to control and change those patterns.

Diane has expressed concerned about her eating patterns. "When I wake up at night, I feel a compulsive urge to eat and I feel I won't be able to fall back asleep if I don't eat," she said. To make it easier to get back to sleep, Diane keeps food by her bedside so that she won't have to go downstairs when she wakes in the middle of the night. This also reduces the chance of disturbing her husband and children's sleep.

In the morning, when she wakes to get the kids ready for school, she has no appetite or interest in food. She tries to force herself to eat what the kids leave over from their breakfast, but usually ends up throwing the leftovers away. As a rule, it's not until the kids return from school and she begins to prepare dinner that her appetite returns. After she and her family eat dinner, she finds herself picking at the food left on the plates. While she eats the leftovers, she feels frustrated and annoyed with herself because she knows that she is overeating. She hopes this extra food will reduce her need to wake up in the middle of the night to eat. Most often it doesn't work.

Eating with Night Eating Syndrome (NES)

The average person begins the day with breakfast, usually sometime before nine o'clock in the morning. Lunch may be eaten around noon or one o'clock in the afternoon. Some people may have a snack in the late afternoon to hold them over until dinner is served. Depending on schedules, most people will eat dinner around six o'clock in the evening, while some may dine as late as nine P.M. After the evening meal, most people may enjoy a dessert, but, in general, they will not eat much more before going to bed. This pattern may vary depending on work and school schedules and cultural preferences. For example, Europeans usually eat their dinners later than Americans. Overall, the average normal eater will eat three meals and occasional snacks during the typical twenty-four-hour day.

As a night eater, this pattern of eating may seem foreign to you. You probably wake up in the morning with little or no appetite. Some night eaters force themselves to eat a little something to try to stay on some type of normal eating schedule. But even if you skip breakfast, you may not have an appetite even at lunchtime. By dinnertime your interest in food has returned and you will eat a great deal during and after dinner. You will not only keep on eating after dinner, but often you may continue eating until late at night; perhaps you even postpone your bedtime just to eat some more food. You may find it hard to fall asleep, and then you may wake up not long after going to sleep, and again later in the night. During these awakenings you may feel not only the need to eat, but also the fear that you will not be able to get back to sleep *unless* you eat some more.

One night eater said, "I could work myself into a panic attack just thinking about having to go to bed without my snacks. When I stay over at other people's homes, I will either sneak something from the fridge and hide it going up the stairs or I'll say good night to everyone and sneak back down and raid the refrigerator. It doesn't make any difference what I eat. It just has to be something."

Eating something before bedtime may make you feel relaxed and satisfied. These feelings help you get to sleep. Your nighttime snacks may continue one or more times during the night. When you wake up in the morning, once again you will have no appetite.

Understanding Eating Patterns

Research at the University of Pennsylvania (Allison et al., Working paper 2004) has demonstrated that obese people who do *not* have NES but who are "normal eaters," (i.e., they eat their meals at traditional mealtimes) had distinct caloric intakes during a typical day. They had a relatively small intake of food at breakfast and two moderately sized meals at midday and early evening. The obese participants who have NES did not report these typical increases in caloric intake at traditional mealtimes. They did not have set mealtimes, and each participant's eating schedule varied.

In this study, the total caloric intake of the night eaters lagged behind the total intake of the "normal eaters" throughout the day. After dinner, though, the intake of the night eaters caught up to the total intake of the normal eaters and kept rising throughout the night, while the caloric intake of the normal eaters leveled off.

As you can see in the graph in figure 2.1, the control subjects (the normal eaters) consumed large amounts of calories around the noon hour and again around the dinner hour. The night eating patients did not exhibit these elevations in their caloric intake. Their graphed line looks a lot smoother, because, on average, they ate at different times throughout the day. They generally ate dinner, and you can see an elevation there. You can also notice that their food intake was much greater than that of the controls after dinner—the night eater's caloric intake line is much higher, and it does not drop as sharply during the nighttime hours.

You, like the night eaters in this study, may have no set mealtimes during the day, except for your pattern of snacking in the evening and at night. In the same study described above, persons without NES ate less than 10 percent of their total daily calories after dinner. However, the night eaters ate about a third of their total daily calories after dinner.

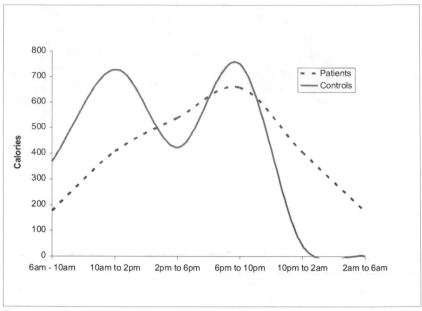

Figure 2.1: Caloric intake of NES patients versus caloric intake of control subjects.

This eating pattern is a key behavior of NES. As a typical night eater, you will find that it is a difficult pattern to overcome, but there are some ways of breaking this cycle. The first is to become more aware of *what* and *when* you are eating.

The Food Diary

In addition to keeping the thought journal discussed in chapter 1, it is an excellent idea to keep a food diary. To keep a record of what you eat, you can use a separate section of the same journal you started in chapter 1, or you can keep a separate food journal. By using a daily food diary, you can track what, when, and how much you are eating. If you carry your journal with you during your day, you can keep a record of everything that goes into your mouth. This is basic information you will need to succeed at changing your eating habits. Remember, knowledge is power.

Try it. Try keeping track of everything you eat for a week. Use the page from John's food diary shown in figure 2.2 as your model.

Time	Food/Beverage Consumed	Quantity	Calories
10 A.M.	English muffin	1 muffin	140
	Grape jelly	2 tsps.	36
	Coffee, no sugar or milk	8 fl. oz.	0
1 P.M.	Tuna fish for sandwich	6 oz.	150
	Whole-wheat bread	2 slices	150
	Mayonnaise	1 tbs.	100
	Lettuce	1 leaf	3
	Tomato	1 slice	5
	Potato chips	1 oz. bag	150
	Cola	20 fl. oz.	250
6 P.M.	Pepperoni pizza	3 slices	930
	Iced tea, sweetened	12 fl. oz.	150
8 P.M.	Vanilla ice cream	1 cup	300
11 P.M.	Chocolate chip cookies	3	180
1 A.M.	Potato chips	1 oz.	150
3 A.M.	Peanut butter	3 tbs.	315
		Total calories:	3009

Figure 2.2: John's food diary.

Using John's diary as an example for our discussion, you can see that John eats quite a large number of calories. Even if he exercises moderately on a regular basis, his caloric intake exceeds recommended levels. Just as the research at the University of Pennsylvania found, John's food diary shows that he ate just over 30 percent of his food after dinner. One of your goals should be to identify this percentage for your own eating habits on average during your week. Notice, too, that John consumes only about 17 percent of his total food intake in the morning. Perhaps this percentage is close to your own morning intake of food. If this is so, your eventual goal should be to increase the percentage of the total daily calories that you eat in the morning. To do this, start your own food diary now. Keep track of everything that you eat for a week to see what your typical eating patterns look like. We have provided some tips for starting and maintaining your diary in the section below.

How to Fill Out Your Food Diary

- Record each meal or snack immediately after you eat it.

- Record the time you eat each meal or snack.

- Record beverages in fluid ounces (fl. oz.).

- Record number and size (sm., med., lg.) for items such as bread, chips, fruits, and snacks.

- Record weights in ounces (oz.) for meat, fish, cheese, etc. (if unknown, give approximate dimensions: length x width x thickness). Specify if chicken is with or without skin. An easy rule to follow is that 3 ounces of meat is approximately the size of a deck of playing cards or about the size of your palm.

- Record in cups (c.) for rice, cereal, soup, and canned fruits.

- Record in teaspoons (tsp.) or tablespoons (tbs.) for jelly, sugar, sauces, etc.

- Measure your favorite bowl, mug, or cup with a measuring cup to get a general idea of how much you are eating of your usual foods, such as cereal, coffee, ice cream, etc.

Figuring Out Your Caloric Needs

Dietary Reference Intakes (DRIs) are daily nutrient recommendations reported by the Institute of Medicine based on the individual's sex and age. Dietary reference intakes stress the importance of a balanced diet and that calorie consumption should be individualized based on age, height, sex, and level of physical activity. They also stress the importance of exercise (Dietary Reference Intakes 2001).

What Is a Calorie?

The calorie is a measure of energy that is available for the body to use. You need to consume a certain number of calories to maintain your weight and energy level. In general, the recommended daily caloric intake for healthy women is 1800 to 2200 calories and for healthy men it is 2000 to 2500. Your level of physical activity will help to pinpoint the caloric intake that is appropriate for you. If you do not exercise and have a sedentary lifestyle, you should aim for the lower number in those ranges. If you exercise regularly and have an active lifestyle, you may want to aim toward the upper limit.

Staying healthy depends not only on how many calories you consume, but also where those calories come from. To meet your body's daily energy and nutritional needs, the Dietary Reference Intakes suggest that adults should consume 45 to 65 percent of their calories from carbohydrates, 20 to 35 percent from fat, and 10 to 20 percent from protein.

How Calories Affect Weight Loss and Gain

Think of your calorie intake like a bank balance. To gain a pound, you must eat 3500 calories more than your body needs to function. This means that if you eat an extra 500 calories per day, you will gain one pound in a week. An extra 500 calories per day means eating an extra peanut butter sandwich or two 20-fluid-ounce regular sodas per day. On the other hand, to lose a pound a week means that you must consume 500 calories less per day than your body needs. If you eat more than you plan, or, in banking terms, deposit more calories than your body needs, you must plan to make a withdrawal by exercising or decreasing your next deposit to make up for the extra calories you ate. Most night eaters compensate for the extra calories deposited overnight by not eating breakfast. We will work with you to change this pattern.

Tips for Keeping Track of Your Food Intake

At this point, you may be thinking, "I can record my foods during the day, but how will I be able to do that at night?" You may be totally aware of your nighttime eating episodes, or you may feel groggy and half-asleep. Your ability to write down the foods that you eat will depend on your level of awareness during each episode. As mentioned in chapter 1, if you have nocturnal sleep-related disorder (NS-RED, described in more detail in chapter 5), then you are sleepwalking and may not be able to record your food except from the evidence of crumbs or wrappers that you find the following morning. Here are some tips that will help you.

Exercise: Tips to Keep Track of What You Eat

- Keep scrap paper and a pen on the kitchen counter, kitchen table, or wherever you usually eat.

- At first, you may find it too difficult to write down what you are eating when you are up at night. If so, keep a small container or basket on your counter for used wrappers or food packaging, so you can record what you have eaten more accurately the next day.

- Enlist the aid of your family or roommates to help you become aware of what you are eating.

- Pre-measure some of your snacks. At this point, we are just trying to raise your awareness about your patterns of eating. Pre-measuring your usual snacks will make it easier to get a good "snapshot" of your nighttime eating habits.

These details will help you to estimate the nutritional and caloric content of your food. To estimate your calories, we recommend that you use the food packaging information to help you record how many servings you have eaten and how many calories are in each serving. This information can be found on the back or side of the box, tin, or wrapper of nearly all packaged foods. Don't forget items that may seem small but can really add to your total intake, such as mayonnaise or butter, candy, soft drinks, sport drinks, or fruit drinks.

We also recommend that you purchase a book or consult nutritional Web pages for caloric and nutritional information. In addition, there are several sources of information listed in Resources section at the back of this book. By writing down this information, you will begin to see your usual pattern of eating, along with your total daily caloric intake. You will also be able to determine what proportion of your total food intake you are eating at night.

After recording what and when you have eaten for a week, ask yourself these questions.

Exercise: What and When Do You Eat?

• WHAT are you eating? Foods high in carbohydrates and fats? Enough fruits and vegetables? How much protein? How many sugary drinks, fruit juices, or glasses of water?

• WHEN are you eating? Three regular meals? Snacks all day long? Or several small meals? Are you eating most of your calories in the morning, afternoon, evening, or at night?

You may notice that recording what you eat influences the amount of food you consume. There is good reason for this. Many weight-loss programs use food diaries as an essential part of their programs, because keeping such a diary has been proven to increase the total amount of weight people lose. Food diaries raise your awareness of your food choices, and keeping this kind of record is the only surefire way to know how many calories you are consuming. Writing down calories may seem time-consuming and difficult at first, but just as with any new task, the longer you do it, the faster and easier it will become.

Food Choices and Meal Planning

Did you know that for every gram of fat or oil products, you consume nine calories, while for every gram of carbohydrate or protein, you consume only four calories? This does not mean you should cut out all the fat from your diet, but you should try to eat lean meats, such as skinless poultry (light meat from chicken and turkey) and nonfried fish. You should also try to use vegetable or olive oil or nonfat cooking sprays instead of butter or lard when cooking. Mayonnaise should be avoided if possible, and a low-fat substitute should be used instead.

The food pyramid from the United States Department of Agriculture (USDA) is a useful tool to guide your daily food choices (see figure 2.3). It encourages you to eat six to eleven servings of breads, cereal, rice, and pasta a day. Be careful to make healthy choices, such as whole-wheat products, brown rice, and other nonbleached flour items. These products often may be

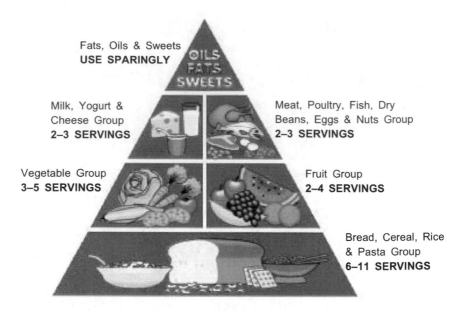

Fats, Oils & Sweets
USE SPARINGLY

OILS
FATS
SWEETS

Milk, Yogurt &
Cheese Group
2–3 SERVINGS

Meat, Poultry, Fish, Dry
Beans, Eggs & Nuts Group
2–3 SERVINGS

Vegetable Group
3–5 SERVINGS

Fruit Group
2–4 SERVINGS

Bread, Cereal, Rice
& Pasta Group
6–11 SERVINGS

Figure 2.3. The Food Pyramid.

more expensive, but they do not contain the refined sugars and man-made preservatives that the processed grain products have.

According to the food pyramid, one serving from the grain group at the bottom of the pyramid is the equivalent of eating one slice of bread or a half a cup of cereal, pasta, or rice. There is a very important point to attend to here. Note that these amounts are much smaller portions than most Americans consume in a typical meal. Therefore, the guideline for the grain group does *not* mean that you should eat these foods six to eleven times in a day. It means that you should eat only six to eleven servings in total. For example, if you ate two slices of bread as part of a sandwich, you have just eaten two servings from the grain group.

Portion Control

The same idea about controlling your food portions should be applied to each of the different categories of the food pyramid. Most Americans typically eat about six (or more) ounces of steak or chicken per dinner. This represents two servings of meat; the amount that is recommended in the food pyramid. So, if you will be having a six-ounce (or larger) serving of meat at your evening meal, you may want to eat a salad, a healthy pasta or rice dish, or a small portion of meat at lunch. Keep in mind that some foods will count in more than one category on the food pyramid. For example, you may be surprised to know that only ten French fries equals one vegetable serving, as well as a helping of fat!

A recent study (Allison et al., Working paper 2004) has found that night eaters consume a higher proportion of protein at night than normal eaters, perhaps because they are eating convenience snacks. Convenience snacks are often leftover meats or peanut butter. In chapters 8 and 9, we will target the food choices you make at night so that you can slowly decrease both the amount of food and the total calories that you consume during the night.

Dieting and NES

Have you tried dieting, only to fail because you still feel compelled to get up and eat at night? You may be able to restrict what you eat during the day, but feel as if you have no control over your night eating. Researchers at the Obesity Research Center in New York City suggest that when people with NES restrict their calories to low levels, this may actually increase their eating at night. In the case study of one night eater, these researchers provided a very low-calorie diet during the day, totaling about 600 calories, versus a more usual intake of 1800 calories. They found that one night eater ate more sandwiches at night after his food had been restricted during the day (Aronoff et al. 1994).

Have you tried to restrict your caloric intake to 1000 calories a day or less? Very low-calorie diets have been shown to help people lose weight rapidly, but very rarely do people sustain the weight lost this way.

The Atkins diet is currently enjoying enormous popularity as a means of weight loss. This popularity has resulted to a considerable degree from a paper published by a colleague in our research group at the University of Pennsylvania (Foster et al. 2003). Large numbers of night eaters struggle with obesity and may wish to try the Atkins diet. However the nutritional background used in developing the NES program was the classic low-fat diet. As a result, the two approaches cannot really be used at the same time.

We suggest that you not diet while you are trying to get your night eating under control. Following a popular diet while you are trying to change your eating patterns may work at cross-purposes and end up frustrating you when you find neither your night eating nor your unwanted pounds are gone. Our goal is to help you establish regular daytime eating habits so that you are able to lose weight, if appropriate, with a more routine and controlled eating schedule.

> *Kristin struggled with anorexia nervosa as a teenager and was insecure about her weight and body image. As she began her recovery, she found herself starting to eat at night. Now she barely eats anything throughout the day, knowing that she will inevitably wake up and eat throughout the night. She usually remembers what she eats, unless she has taken a sleep aid. When she takes a sleeping pill, she feels groggy and has trouble knowing whether she is dreaming or if her eating is real. She has sought help for her sleeping and eating problems at residential treatment centers, where she was able to stop her night eating for a short time. However, her unhealthy night eating routine returned once she arrived home after treatment.*

Kristin, perhaps like you, needs to learn how to control her eating in her home environment. She feels frustrated that traditional residential eating and sleep disorders centers haven't helped her NES. Neither type of center directly addressed her problem. But keeping a diary may make her aware of her eating patterns in her home, which in the short term may cause her some distress. In the long term it should help to initiate changes in her behavior and eating patterns over the twenty-four hours of a day.

Exercise: Let's Plan Your Meals

Do you plan your meals at the beginning of the day (or by the week), or do you eat random foods at random times? Start to answer this by thinking about your usual eating habits and examining them in greater detail as you keep your food diary.

1. **How many days per week do you eat breakfast?** Even people who are not physically hungry in the morning, will benefit from eating a healthy breakfast. Those who eat a healthy breakfast can resist impulsive snacking more easily, and they actually lose more weight in clinical weight loss programs (Schlundt et al. 1992).

2. **Do you eat a midmorning snack?** If you do not have an appetite in the morning when you wake up, you may start to feel physically hungry by midmorning. If you have not eaten breakfast, you may want to have a nutritious morning snack, including a piece of fruit or a breakfast bar.

3. **When do you eat lunch?** Do you have a usual lunchtime? Or do you grab something on the run? The more established you can make your mealtimes, the easier your body will be able to adjust to a new eating schedule. Remember that it can take up to three months to turn a new behavior into a habit, so hang in there.

4. **Do you have a midafternoon snack?** If so, how late in the afternoon is it? Does your appetite for a snack get activated late in the day? Or does your snack get to be so large that you are not hungry for an evening meal around 6:00 P.M.?

5. **What time is your evening meal? How large is it?** If you are a typical night eater, you will probably say that this is your largest meal of the day, as it is for many Americans. You may still want to keep this meal as your largest of the day, especially while you are beginning to try to eat earlier in the day. However, as you work on shifting some of your calories to lunch and breakfast, you will want to cut back on the total amount of calories you eat at supper.

   On the other hand, you may not eat a regular evening meal. Instead, you may eat a succession of snacks starting at the time that most people eat dinner. At this time of day, it's important to eat a balanced meal that will fill you up and satisfy your physical hunger. If you do not enjoy cooking, or if you live alone, you may find it difficult to eat a balanced meal every evening. If either of these possibilities—not liking to cook or living alone—describes your situation, then right now is a good time to visit your grocery store and explore new food options. You will be surprised at how little time it takes to prepare and cook fresh fish, make yourself a salad with precooked chicken, or steam some fresh or frozen vegetables. Each of these foods takes no more than fifteen minutes to prepare.

6. **Do you eat several snacks at night or do you plan to have one snack?** If you typically take a bag of chips or popcorn with you to the couch as you watch television, you may eat half of the bag before you even realize it. Stop this pattern. Instead, plan out or pre-measure the amount you want to eat for your snack. Chew each bite, and pay attention to the taste as you eat. If you eat without noticing the taste of your food, you will not enjoy the experience as much, and you will not give your body a chance to feel full. If you still feel hungry after eating your planned snack, wait a while before you go back for more. It takes between ten and thirty minutes for your body to inform your brain that you are full. If you still feel hungry, then you may want to eat something else, but be sure to pre-measure a specific amount, and remember to wait at least ten minutes after you finish it before checking yourself to see whether you are still hungry.

7. **When you wake up at night, do you feel physically hungry?** When you write down what you are eating at night in your food diary, make a note of how hungry you are. What is your level of physical hunger? You can use a quick estimate, such as the following scale, ranging from "0" being not at all hungry to "10" being extremely hungry. If you are not physically hungry, then a snack low in calories or a drink of water may be enough, instead of eating a whole sandwich. This is something to experiment with to see whether you can become more aware of your eating behaviors at night. In chapter 8, you will learn more about how to make yourself aware of your actions earlier and earlier when you wake up and are feeling groggy.

So far, you've learned some tips to help you become more aware of your eating patterns over an entire twenty-four-hour period. Normalizing your eating patterns by eating breakfast and balanced meals is a good start, but you will have to make other lifestyle changes before you can win your battle with NES. Resuming a more normal pattern of eating probably won't be sufficient to end your late night eating, but it is certainly a necessary condition in the process.

This Chapter's Goals

- Start a food diary and keep track of your usual eating habits—day and night—for one week.

- At the end of one week, examine your total calorie amounts and the proportion of food that you ate in the morning, midday, and at night.

- After this first week, continue to keep your food diary and begin to shift some of your caloric intake to earlier in the day.

CHAPTER 3

Sleeping Patterns: Up All Night?

If you have night eating syndrome, for you the night may be the most difficult part of the twenty-four hours of a day. Knowing that you probably will face another night of troubled sleep can cause anxiety as the evening nears. Moreover, like your eating patterns, the sleeping patterns you experience as a night eater are very different from those of the average person.

According to one night eater, "The pattern is always the same. . . . I get up about an hour to an hour and a half after falling asleep, and then I eat. It's a terrible, terrible thing, and it's not easy to control. Right now, the only way I can control it is to have my husband literally lock me in the bedroom at night and hide the key. I know this sounds extreme, but it's the only way to keep me in the bedroom and not headed for the kitchen." *Willpower doesn't work. Surrender*

We often hear from our patients that many of you wake up at similar times every night. One sufferer complained, "I fall asleep fairly easily; however, I wake every hour nearly on the hour. Sometimes I get up and smoke a cigarette or I read in my effort not to eat. This can go on for two to three times, and then I give in—and I eat. Then I sleep like a baby." The longer you have been getting up at night to eat, the more often, or severe, your night eating may have become, and the more "regular" your "irregular" eating pattern may be. *Since I got sober?*

The Stages of Sleep

Normal sleep is divided into two segments, nonrapid eye movement sleep (NREM) and rapid eye movement sleep (REM). You may be more familiar with REM sleep, which is the stage when you are dreaming. Yet, you also may be aware of NREM sleep as the time you are most often moving around and repositioning your body.

Nonrapid Eye Movement Sleep

Nonrapid eye movement sleep is actually divided into four stages. With each stage your sleep becomes deeper and deeper. The four stages are described below.

Stage 1: Falling asleep. Only a small proportion—approximately ten minutes—of your total sleep time is spent in stage 1. During this time you are moving in and out of sleep and can be awakened easily. Your muscles relax and your eyes move slowly. Stage 1 sleep is usually the period when you experience those sudden leg or arm jerks that may awaken you. While in stage 1, you also may experience what are technically called *hypnogogic hallucinations*, when you may see vivid visions and colors or hear voices. To better understand stage 1 sleep, think back to when you've nodded off in school or at a meeting, and you suddenly jerked yourself awake. You were in stage 1 sleep.

Stage 2: Light sleep. Usually, you will spend about thirty minutes in stage 2 before you enter a deeper sleep stage. As an adult, you spend about half of your total sleeping time in stage 2. During stage 2, your eye movements stop and your brain activity, often measured as *brain waves,* slows down. Stage 2 is also characterized by quick bursts of brain activity, known as *spindles.*

Stages 3 and 4: Deep sleep. These stages are also referred to as *slow wave sleep,* because the brain activity (or wave patterns) is much slower. This sleep is much deeper than during stages 1 and 2. Your body uses these final stages of NREM sleep to recuperate physically from the day's efforts. During stage 3 sleep, your brain waves slow down even more than in stage 2. The waves produced in stage 3 are called *delta waves,* and they contain smaller, faster waves within the slow waves. Stage 4 exhibits almost exclusively delta, or very slow, waves. During slow wave sleep, your muscles are deeply relaxed, and there is no eye movement. Most of your slow wave sleep occurs in the earlier part of the night. Curiously, sleepwalking takes place during slow wave sleep, and if you wake up from stage 3 or 4 sleep, you will feel groggy and disoriented.

Rapid Eye Movement Sleep

During REM sleep, sometimes referred to as *stage 5 sleep*, your eyes move very rapidly and your mind engages in the complex, vivid imagery you know as dreams. But, in contrast to NREM sleep, the nerves controlling your muscles are turned off in REM sleep, in effect paralyzing your body so that you do not actually act out your dreams. This strange distinction between the activity in the mind and the inactivity of the body has caused REM sleep to be called *paradoxical sleep.*

Along with your mind, your autonomic nervous system, which automatically controls your breathing and heart, is aroused. So, at the same time that your muscles are limp and motionless, your heart beats faster and your blood pressure rises. Typically, people experience these five stages of sleep, the sleep cycle, for about 90 minutes, but each sleep cycle (consisting of stages 1 through 4 and REM) may last as long as 120 minutes.

The Sleep Cycle

The *normal sleep cycle* consists of alternating NREM and REM cycles, repeating every ninety minutes throughout the night. These cycles occur between four and six times a night; yet as sleep continues, the proportion of deep sleep—stages 3 and 4—decreases, and the amount of sleep in stages 1, 2, and REM sleep increases. Toward morning, a REM period may occur while you are waking up, which is why your last dream of the night may be influenced by your surroundings and may be the easiest to recall.

Factors That Affect Sleep

Many factors can affect the sleep cycle, including ingesting alcohol, drugs, or caffeine, experiencing stress, or other sleep disorders (see chapter 5). Age also affects this cycle. Young children need a great deal of sleep that may last for ten or more hours a day. Children have far more REM sleep than do adults. As much as a third to a half of their time spent sleeping consists of REM sleep.

Adults usually sleep six to eight hours a night, depending on work and social schedules, and less of their sleep time is devoted to REM—perhaps 20 to 30 percent. Total sleep time continues to diminish as people age, and elderly persons usually sleep less continuously than young ones; that is, they frequently wake up during the night. This decreased sleep time involves both REM and NREM sleep. Most elderly people report that they do not sleep as soundly as they used to and that their sleep is not as restful as it had been in their midlife years and earlier.

NES and Sleep

Although it is believed that patients with NES typically follow the patterns of sleep in the usual cycles described above, you probably know that your sleep is quite disturbed and not as continuous as the description above suggests. In this regard, one patient said, "I wake up approximately every one and a half to two hours with an overwhelming desire to eat. Most nights I wake up four or five times and I eat sweets, cookies, or cereal at about three of those awakenings. Some nights, though, I will eat each time I wake up." This patient has described a severe case of NES. You and many others with NES may awaken and eat only occasionally. Nevertheless, any eating at night on a regular basis is disruptive and distressing. So what is "typical" for night eaters?

Getting Out of Bed

We explored this question by asking night eaters and non–night eaters, matched for weight and age, to use a detailed diary to keep track of their eating and sleeping habits at home for a week. We found that, on average, night eaters get up out of bed 1.7 times per night, or about 12 times in a week, and they eat 1.4 times per night, or about 9.5 times in a week. If you follow this usual pattern, it means that you may eat more than 80 percent of the time when you wake up and get out of bed.

By comparison, non–night eaters awoke and got out of bed 0.6 times per night, or roughly once every other night (O'Reardon et al., Working paper 2004). Especially worthy of note is the fact that not one person in the comparison group ate even once when he or she got out of bed!

In order to confirm the study participants' self-reports of awakenings, we had them wear motion sensors. These small instruments, worn on the wrist like a watch, were extremely helpful for demonstrating that the study participants were accurately reporting the times that they got out of bed. Comparing the sensors to the diaries, the motion sensors showed increased activity about 90 percent of the times that participants documented their getting up, an unusually high degree of agreement.

Duration of Time Asleep

Bedtimes for both NES patients and control participants were almost the same. Both groups, on average, went to sleep between 11:30 P.M. and midnight and woke up between 7:00 A.M. and 7:30 A.M. (O' Reardon et al., Working paper 2004). Of course, these times are averages and there was a great deal of difference among the participants as to these times. Your bedtime and wake-up time may vary as well. In general, though, we found that NES patients woke up in the morning about half an hour later than the control group, perhaps making up for the time they spent out of bed while eating.

For a long time we thought that the disturbed sleep of night eaters reflected a disorder in the biological rhythms that govern sleep and waking. Just recently we've discovered that this is not at all the case; the biological rhythm that controls sleep in night eaters is not at all disordered, but rather it functions perfectly well. This good news resulted from our studies here at the University of Pennsylvania of the bedtimes for both the night eaters and the control participants (O'Reardon et al., Working paper 2004). The surprisingly similar times for going to sleep and waking up mean that the biological rhythms of sleep in night eaters do not differ from those of the average person.

Disturbed Sleep

Although the onset of sleep and the total amount of time in bed were similar for night eaters and control participants, the amount of restful sleep was quite different. The sleep diaries and motion sensors told the distressing stories of the night eaters. The sleep of the night eaters was far more disturbed than the control participants' sleep. The night eaters got out of bed during the night more often than the controls. They also got out of bed much earlier.

For example, the first time they got up occurred at 1:20 A.M., less than two hours after they had fallen asleep. Of course, we could not measure those times when participants woke up but did not get out of bed. But because you must get out of bed (or at least sit up) before up you can eat, accounts of waking up but not getting out of bed didn't seem essential for a good description of night eating.

Night eaters got up for a second time at 2:45 A.M., on average. In contrast, the controls (non–night eaters) not only got out of bed less often than the night eaters, but the first time that they got out of bed averaged around 3:00 A.M. By this time, the night eaters had already been out of bed twice, and most often had eaten both times. It was rare for the controls to get up a second time and, as noted, they did not eat on any occasion.

The implications of these early awakenings are still being studied. However, we do know that it is unusual, at the very least, to experience awakenings as early in the night as the night eaters do. You may first wake up an hour or two into your sleep, and if you are able to remember what you did when you awoke, you have probably awakened from stages 1, 2, or REM sleep.

On the other hand, you may awake feeling groggy, with a reduced awareness of your actions. The less conscious awareness you have when you wake, the more likely you are to have awakened from slow wave sleep during stages 3 and 4. This range of awareness will vary depending on the stage of sleep you were in when you awoke. Some people say that they do not feel quite their normal selves when they wake at night. One classic night eater described these feelings by saying, "I'm not sure I'm the same person when I am up eating. I swear like a sailor and would hit anyone who tried to stop me or got in my way—even to talk to me."

Polysomnography

In addition to the studies of night eaters in their homes, we brought a smaller group of them and their matched control group counterparts (who were selected to be similar to the NES patients in age and BMI) into the hospital for a more intensive study that lasted for three days and nights. During this time we used a technique called *polysomnography* (PSG) to measure their sleep. To use this technique, electrodes are placed on key points of the subjects' heads, and they are asked to sleep with the electrodes on, while their sleep is monitored. If you have ever had your sleep studied, you may be familiar with this method.

The PSG measures brain waves (brain activity), breathing pat terns, and muscle and limb movements. It also takes very accurate measures of the time of sleep onset, times of nighttime awakenings, and the time of morning awakening. Polysomnography monitors the stages of sleep that the subject passes through, and the pattern that is created over the course of the night is called the *sleep architecture* of the individual who was studied.

We measured the patients' sleep for two nights, using the first night as an adjustment period during which the patients became accustomed to the hospital. By the second night, sleep patterns typically return to a person's usual routine. Patients brought their favorite foods to the hospital and placed them on a table beside their bed so they could continue their usual pattern of night eating. Although these studies were much more precise than those of the patients in their homes, they confirmed the results of the home studies. Thus, there were no differences in sleep onset, morning awakening, or total sleep time between night eaters and control participants (Dinges et al. unpublished observations).

However, in the critical measure known as *sleep efficiency*, which is the proportion of restful sleep to the total amount of time spent between going to bed and getting up in the morning, the night eaters demonstrated a much lower proportion: only 65 percent compared to 82 percent for the control subjects.

One fascinating finding from the hospital study concerned the difference between what the night eaters and the control participants did when they awoke. Night eaters ate 80 percent of the times when they were aware of waking. In striking contrast, only one of the fifteen control subjects ate upon awakening.

The hospital study provided a further important piece of information. That is, the 80 percent eating rate of the night eaters showed that night eating can take place in unfamiliar surroundings, including one as unusual and sterile as a hospital room. Many night eaters who report that they continue to eat at night even when on vacation or at a friend's house corroborate this finding. Although the eating may be somewhat reduced when the environment is changed, it still takes place.

One man who traveled frequently for his job tried to find lodging only in motels or hotels where he would have easy access to a minibar with food already stocked. If he could not find a room like this, he would get up and wander the halls looking for a vending machine so he could get crackers and cookies. If he couldn't find a vending machine, in desperation he would drink water and fall back to sleep with difficulty. He reported that after falling asleep under these circumstances, he dreamt of the cookies that he had not been able to find.

Other night eaters bring food to their hotel rooms to make sure that something is always available. You may have experienced this problem yourself in a friend's or relative's home, where you roamed through the strange house in the middle of the night searching for food. For some, the drive to eat overpowers their reluctance to "get caught," and they search until they find food. For others, this means that they can't eat, which usually results in having trouble falling asleep and staying asleep.

Some night eaters eat whenever they sleep, even after a short nap. One night eater said, "I avoid naps, because if I sleep for even an hour, I always eat when I wake up. If anyone tries to talk to me right after a nap, I want to kill him or her. All I want is food, whether it tastes good or not."

Insomnia

For some of you, falling asleep is not a problem, but others may spend a half an hour or more tossing and turning. We used to think that all night eaters experienced this initial insomnia. But that is not the case. We now know that some night eaters do not have this problem. However, enough night eaters do suffer from insomnia to raise the issue of the influence of sleeping pills, both prescription and over-the-counter sleep aids. That's because one obvious response to difficulty in getting to sleep is to take sleeping pills. This is not always a wise move and it may be best to avoid it, if possible.

NES and Sleep Medications

Our survey of night eaters revealed that sleep medications did not really reduce the number of times they got up to eat. In fact, the patients often reported that sleep medications lowered their resistance to eating. For some of them, sleep medications led them to get out of bed to eat more often than usual, and these medications also made them less aware of their eating.

As stated above, waking to eat in the early part of the night is certainly unusual, but waking early in the night under the influence of sleeping pills is even more unusual. There is a more detailed discussion of the biological aspects of NES in chapter 7. A discussion of the influence of medications in treating NES can be found in chapter 11.

Exercise: What You Can Do to Improve Your Sleep Patterns

1. First, go to bed at the same time every night.

2. You are already making entries into your food diary every day. Now you should start keeping track of your bedtimes and awakening times. You can use the same journal to keep track of your sleep patterns.

3. After you have kept a diary of your usual eating behaviors for a week to record your baseline patterns, try to eat more of your caloric intake to earlier in the day.

4. When you are eating more calories earlier in the day, try to reduce the amount of food that you eat during the night.

5. Experiment with the minimum amount of food you need to eat to fall back to sleep. As suggested in chapter 2, premeasure some snacks and try to restrict your night eating only to these foods.

6. Remember, if you are taking sleeping aids or if you tend to wake up out of slow wave sleep, it may be difficult for you to have much awareness of your choices. If this pattern often occurs for you, enlist the help of a bed partner or roommate on a regular basis, if available, to rouse you from your grogginess.

This Chapter's Goals

- Become more aware of your sleeping patterns. Keep an accurate record of your bedtimes and awakening times.

- Pay attention to circumstances that affect the frequency of your night eating. For example, a change of environment might affect your nighttime eating, or the presence of someone who is aware of your night eating could have an effect on your behavior.

- Begin to experiment with reducing your food intake to the minimum amount that will help you fall back to sleep.

CHAPTER 4

How Are You
Feeling Today?

If you suffer from NES, you have undoubtedly been barraged by
a range of negative feelings, emotions, or moods. We will try to
explore the relationship between NES and these feelings, particularly those of depression, guilt, anxiety, anger at oneself, and
embarrassment. The connections between these emotions can be
seen clearly in one patient's statement: "I'm embarrassed about
my lack of control and angry that I'm sabotaging my health.
Despite feeling so lousy, I can't seem to break this pattern of
eating at night."

Shame

    Let's begin our exploration with depression, which is the
mood most consistently associated with NES. It is also the
emotional state that has been subjected to the greatest amount of
study.

Depression

Everyone has felt depressed at one time or other and, conse-
quently, there are many ordinary terms to describe the feeling.
Some people say they are "sad," "blue," or "down in the dumps";
others prefer "unhappy," "discontented," or "gloomy." No matter
what they choose to call it, feelings of depression affect many

depression makes life unmanageable. Solness doesn't

people at a *subclinical* level. Sad feelings exist, but they are not interfering with daily functions.

The severity of a depressed mood varies widely, along with its frequency and duration. For some people, a depressed mood is a rare event and may never be very severe. For others, depression is a serious problem. If it is severe, it can interfere with their ability to work, with their personal interactions, such as with family and friends, and with their ability to feel pleasant and comfortable feelings. When depression is severe and lasts longer than two weeks, it may be diagnosed as a psychiatric disorder at the clinical level. Clinical depression may affect up to 10 percent of all adult Americans in their lifetimes (Kessler et al. 1994).

Symptoms of Depression

Some of the symptoms you may experience include the following (DSM-IV-TR 2000):

- Feeling sad, empty, or depressed

- Loss of interest or pleasure in most daily and social activities

- Significant weight loss or loss of appetite, or the opposite, significant weight gain or increase in appetite

- Sleeping significantly fewer or significantly more hours every day

- Feeling agitated or, the opposite, talking or moving more lethargically than usual

- Fatigue or loss of energy

- Feeling as if you are worthless or feeling guilty about things you have done or not done

- Difficulty thinking, concentrating, or making decisions about everyday concerns, such as what to eat or what to wear

- Reoccurring thoughts of death or having a plan for taking your life

If you experience symptoms of depression that last for at least two consecutive weeks, you may be experiencing what is called a *major depressive episode*. To be diagnosed with a major depressive episode, you must experience at least one of the first two bulleted symptoms and at least five of the remaining seven. If you experience fewer symptoms, you probably feel depressed at a subclinical level.

These symptoms must noticeably interfere with your daily life. Usually, other people, such as close family or friends, can observe such changes in your behavior. For example, you may have trouble getting out of bed in the morning and deciding what to wear and what to eat, and you may have to struggle to leave the house. Housework is neglected, and you don't feel like seeing your friends and family. The activities and relationships that formerly gave you pleasure no longer bring you much enjoyment. Others may notice that you walk, talk, and generally move more slowly than usual. Or they may observe the opposite in your behavior; that is, you seem fidgety and restless and cannot sit still for very long.

There are other changes in your functioning that accompany depression. Your interest in sex may decline, which can upset your husband, wife, or partner. Others may notice that you seem increasingly irritable. When you are depressed, you usually don't have a lot of patience for dealing with others, because often you would rather be left alone. This can create problems.

Your friends and family may try to help you by remaining friendly and interested in how you are doing, but your responses may be only short comments or you may angrily refuse to go out or even talk. The longer you experience depression, the less your friends and family will try to engage you, simply because after a while they get tired of being rebuffed. Thus, the more depressed you get, and the longer you stay that way, the more isolated you can become.

Depression Symptoms Caused by Other Conditions

Some of the symptoms listed above may result from medical illnesses or from drug use, so the pattern of symptoms for major depression must be considered in light of any medications or recent illnesses you may have experienced. Major depression is also distinct from grieving over the death of a loved one, unless the grieving period extends for a very long time and significantly interferes with your daily functioning. In this case, grief can evolve into a major depressive episode.

Depression and NES

In our studies at the University of Pennsylvania, we found that about 45 percent of our NES participants had experienced a major depressive episode at some point in their lives, and that an additional 30 percent had experienced other forms of depression. This was much higher than the 18 percent of the control participants who had experienced major depression (Allison et al., Working paper 2004). Other researchers also have found that NES patients report a depressed mood (Gluck, Geliebter, and Satov 2001; Napolitano et al. 2001). Self-esteem is also usually low in night eaters, which can interfere with your ability to reach out to others and begin your journey to recovery (Gluck, Geliebter, and Satov 2001).

There are different patterns of depression, with the two best-described patterns being the melancholic and the atypical patterns. The pattern usually demonstrated by those with NES differs from both the melancholic and the atypical patterns.

The Melancholic Pattern of Depression

In the *melancholic* form of depression, the mood pattern varies in a distinctive way throughout the day. If you are experiencing this pattern, you usually awaken feeling badly. Mornings often are the low point of your day. The depression lessens throughout the day and it may be significantly relieved by evening. The really bad part of the day is the beginning. It may be very difficult for you to get out of bed and to find the motivation you need to get your day started.

Early morning awakenings (called *terminal insomnia*) are a distinctive characteristic of melancholic depression. These awakenings may occur as much as two to three hours before you need to wake up, and they are very unpleasant. You lie there, worried, anxious, troubled with all kinds of thoughts racing through your mind. You imagine every possible action you might take ending in failure, and you feed your sense of helplessness with your imaginings.

You might think that if someone feels so badly, that person would get out of bed and try to start the day, but that doesn't happen. Instead, you lie in bed, ruminating about troubles that seem both endless and insurmountable, and you feel more and more frightened and helpless. The essence of this kind of depression was captured by F. Scott Fitzgerald, famous author and no stranger to depression, who put the feelings into these well-known words, "In a real dark night of the soul, it is always three o'clock in the morning."

The Atypical Pattern of Depression

The melancholic type of depression is not the only pattern that exists. Another, less common, type is called *atypical depression*. With this type, you experience symptoms of excess. For example, from the symptoms of depression listed above, you would overeat throughout the day (instead of having a lack of appetite) and you would have hypersomnia, that is, you would sleep more than usual (instead of having insomnia). Thus, with atypical depression, you are likely to gain weight and to sleep ten, twelve, or more hours a day. You may also experience a heavy feeling in your arms and legs, as if they were full of lead and hard to move.

With atypical depression, you usually respond well to others' efforts to cheer you up, and you like receiving caring attention. You may, however, also be very sensitive to criticism, which may lead you to avoid being around people who are not aware of and sympathetic to your feelings.

The NES Pattern of Depression

Many people with NES experience a unique pattern of depressed mood. It goes something like this: You may rise from sleep feeling okay, perhaps a bit groggy from getting up to eat during the night. As the day progresses, however, you feel more depressed, possibly by the anticipation of another evening of eating and an unsettled night's sleep.

In our study (Allison et al., Working paper 2004), we found that the moods reported by NES participants over the course of the day were lower than the moods of the control participants before 8 P.M., and after 8 P.M. the moods of NES participants were also more likely to fall than were the moods of the controls. This same fall in mood was also found in an earlier study (Birketvedt et al. 1999).

Although this NES pattern is similar to atypical depression, that is, the person's mood deteriorates during the day, it is distinct from this condition. With atypical depression, the sufferer overeats, but not with the *delayed circadian pattern* (this means not eating in the morning and eating increasingly more later in the day) that occurs in NES. Furthermore, with atypical depression, sufferers sleep significantly more than usual. But we found in our clinical studies that, on the contrary, NES participants slept a comparable amount to the control participants who were enrolled in the study. (All participants and controls kept a sleep diary and wore a motion sensor to estimate their sleep patterns.)

Both groups reported bedtimes at approximately 11:30 P.M. and a morning wake-up time around 7:00 A.M. (O'Reardon et al., Working paper 2004). Most of our NES participants worked full-time jobs; clearly, they were not napping during the day, as people with atypical depression often do. They weren't experiencing the terminal insomnia typical of melancholic depression. So, although the drop in mood throughout the day may be similar to the atypical depression pattern, the mood pattern most commonly experienced by NES sufferers is actually quite distinct. In part III, we will discuss ways to help you overcome your feelings of depression.

Helpful Hint: Physical Activity

If the symptoms listed above under "Depression" seem to fit your situation and depression has been bothering you, try exercising. If you have not exercised in the past, walking for a total of thirty minutes every day would be best, but start slowly, walking three to four days each week. If you cannot squeeze thirty minutes of walking into your busy schedule, park further away from your workplace, use the stairs instead of the elevator, or try to take three ten-minute walks during the day.

During these walks, exert enough effort to raise your heartbeat, but be careful not to overdo it if you are not accustomed to exercise. Not only will exercise help your mood, but also if you are struggling with your weight, it will help you get into shape faster. Note that, although we enthusiastically recommend that you start an exercise program, always consult your physician before starting an exercise routine.

Guilt

Guilt is the feeling that makes you look at yourself and your actions in a negative light. Guilt makes you feel intrinsically bad and nonaccepting of yourself. It may be one of the most

[handwritten: Futility of guilt]

unproductive emotions a human being can experience. It does not motivate you to change or make improvements; it only allows you to dwell on your nonacceptance of your actions.

You may feel guilty about your eating patterns. Most sufferers of eating disorders feel guilty after eating. Those with NES feel guilty mainly about what they ate during the previous evening and night. Some people feel the impact of this guilt more than others. As a rule, guilt generally affects you when you believe that you have done something wrong. So if you believe that you are a bad person because of what you ate, you will probably feel guilty.

[handwritten: eating at night carries heavy weight throughout my day]

Often, guilt carries a religious or spiritual connotation with it, because it invokes an evaluation or judgment about what kind of person you are. For many, this connotation is related to larger, spiritual issues that they may have absorbed as children, by which they may try to live their lives.

Guilt evokes its worst effect when your thoughts turn to persistent shame. Shame causes stress because it is intricately linked to feelings of ineffectiveness. You may not feel capable of coping with the problems in your life; more specifically, you may feel unable to stop your night eating. When you combine this general feeling of ineffectiveness with the absence of social support due to a lack of understanding about your disorder, your feelings of guilt may turn into a heavy, shameful secret. In chapter 7, you will find a discussion about how the stress caused by guilt feelings can affect both your body and your health.

Overcoming Guilty Feelings

If feelings of guilt are gnawing away at your self-esteem, there are several matters to think about and several steps you can take to help yourself either reduce or accept your feelings. These are summarized in the list below.

1. Don't assume too much responsibility either for negative events or feelings. Feeling guilty about your eating actually can activate feeling guilty about other negative events. Don't blame yourself for everything.

2. Basically, you have two choices: (1) you can change whatever is making you feel guilty or (2) you can accept it. Obviously, if you feel guilty about your night eating and you are reading this book, you are taking steps to change

the situation. Although your other option is to accept the condition of having NES—and give up feeling guilty about having it—we hope that you decide that change is your best choice.

3. Perhaps you had a lapse and you ate something you promised yourself you wouldn't eat when you woke up last night. Don't chastise yourself forever. Forgive yourself and set a new goal for the following night. We will discuss forbidden foods and the challenges of incorporating them into your diet in an acceptable way in chapter 9.

4. Use others to help you work through your feelings of guilt. Other people may provide you with different perspectives that may help to ease or even eliminate your feelings of guilt. See chapter 10 for insights about discussing NES with others.

Anxiety

Anxiety is another very common feeling that can be a problem for you. Just as everyone feels depressed from time to time, most of us experience anxiety. This is a normal response, especially in new social situations, job interviews, before getting married, or having a baby. Anxiety around events like these may give you butterflies in your stomach, but the feeling also gives your body energy to mobilize itself and get through whatever lies ahead.

However, some types of anxiety are not so positive. When you worry about a fight you had with your spouse, your finances, or the safety of your children, anxiety can be a very uncomfortable and unsettling feeling. It can affect you adversely, both physically and psychologically.

Common Symptoms of Anxiety

- Increase in or loss of appetite

- Problems sleeping

- Racing heart

- Sweaty palms

- Inability to sit still, restlessness

- Fatigue or exhaustion

- Upset stomach

- Sexual difficulties

- Muscle tension in your neck, face, or shoulders

- Racing thoughts

You may experience many of these symptoms. The more severe they are, the more they interfere with your life. If you feel anxious and worry more than half of the time, or if you experience panic attacks—in which you suddenly feel very frightened or extremely anxious and feel as though something is very wrong with you physically—you should consult a mental health professional. This level of worrying generally has a negative impact on your life and daily functioning and can impair your ability to work and to enjoy life.

Anxious/Agitated Type of NES

For many people, food is a comfort in times of anxiety. However, for others, anxiety makes them feel as though their stomach had been tied into knots, and they can't possibly eat anything when they are worrying. So, how does anxiety affect you and your NES?

Tom's Story

Tom's story may be familiar to you because many NES patients report similar accounts. He has tried a variety of different remedies to stop eating during the night, including using sleep aids, drinking hot milk or herbal tea before bedtime, and making sure he is good and tired before settling into bed. Nevertheless, he often wakes up abruptly an hour or two after going to sleep. He described a specific night to us in this way:

I was suddenly wide awake and in a bad mood. I was not physically hungry, but I was pretty agitated. I just wanted to fall back to sleep, and I knew that eating would do it. The longer I lay there awake, the more anxious and agitated I became. I couldn't stop thinking about the fight I had earlier that day with my boss. It was really bothering me that the situation was left unresolved. The ice cream in the freezer was calling my name, and the longer I went

*without it, the more irritable I became. I couldn't lie still
any longer. I finally got out of bed and gave in to my
urges to eat.*

You can see that Tom, perhaps like you, seeks food at night
when he is plagued by common worries that create anxiety. After
eating, his anxiety is soothed, at least temporarily, and a vicious
cycle of night eating continues. So, how does anxiety affect you
and your NES?

Obsessions and Compulsions

Generally, *obsessions* are thoughts or images that you can't get rid
of—they keep returning to your mind, even when you try to
think about something else. Tom's thoughts about food and about
his boss were obsessive. Thus, obsessions have to do with your
thoughts. *Compulsions*, on the other hand, have to do with behaviors that are usually performed in response to mental obsessions.
Compulsions are urges to perform certain acts over and over
again, such as washing your hands, checking something several
times to make sure you have done it correctly, or counting up to a
certain number before undertaking an action. For people who are
obsessive-compulsive, performing these behaviors generally
brings some psychological relief after they do them. However, the
relief does not last long, and the obsessive thoughts usually
return, followed by the compulsive behaviors.

Most NES sufferers do not have full-blown cases of obsessive compulsive disorder (OCD), but some of the same obsessive
symptoms of that disorder seem to apply to those with NES. For
example, the thoughts that you have during the evening or at
night about the comfort and sleepiness that food will bring are
repetitive. They will cause many of you anxiety, which results in
physical agitation if you do not eat. Thus, the act of eating
becomes the compulsion.

Another patient described how obsessions and compulsions
played a role in initiating his night eating episodes. Michael, a
new father, worried about his daughter while she slept. He had
heard about sudden infant death syndrome (SIDS) and was afraid
that SIDS might strike his little girl. So, during the night, he
would get up and check to see that she was breathing. He usually
drank a glass of water at that time. But drinking water progressed
to eating a snack when he got up. As his daughter grew older, he

no longer worried about SIDS, but he continued to wake up and eat. His behavior became automatic, and he was driven to eat so that he would be able to fall back to sleep. Michael, who was happily married and a successful businessman, continued this pattern for more than thirty years, until he came to see us and enrolled in our research program.

Most of you, like Michael, do not have these types of thoughts and urges to eat during the day (they are confined to nighttime hours and center on your need to comfort yourself with food, so that you can get a good night's sleep), indicating that these thoughts and behaviors are specific to NES.

However, if you are experiencing more pervasive obsessive thoughts or compulsions, for example, having to check that your door is locked ten times every night before going to bed, being unable to leave your house without checking five times every morning to make sure your oven is not lit, or thinking you have been contaminated and need to wash your hands repeatedly, you should consult a mental health professional.

Feeling Angry at Yourself

As with the other emotions discussed in this chapter, probably not one of us is a stranger to anger. Anger can be a healthy response to a real threat, and it can help us let off steam when we feel we have been wronged. However, as with most things in this world, too much anger may affect you negatively, along with those around you.

Persistently feeling angry can affect your health detrimentally. Anger at this level is often called *hostility*. Hostility can foster such serious conditions as a heart attack or stroke. If you are overweight in addition to feeling a chronically high level of hostility, then you are significantly increasing your risk for one of these events.

For those with NES, anger usually comes into play not so much against others as against themselves. You may become appropriately angry with others during the day, but the anger you feel toward yourself can be linked to your evaluation of your eating patterns and the effects those patterns have had on your weight and health. Many of the people we study say that they feel as though they have totally lost control over their eating at night. And although their night eating caused them anxiety when it first began, for some people that anxiety turned into a permanent state of anger at themselves. They are angry that they are overweight, angry that they can't get a full night of sleep without eating, and angry that this pattern has afflicted them for no reason that they can understand.

Embarrassment

Night eaters may be embarrassed about their eating patterns for many reasons. You may have told someone you feel close to about your difficulties and received a less-than-supportive response. You may feel as though you have lost control of your eating, and this may have had a negative impact on your self-esteem and your concept of yourself as a person. You also may be ashamed that you take others' food during your driven urges to eat. Finally, you may be embarrassed by the weight you've gained as a result of your eating patterns.

Amanda told us of her embarrassment in the following situation, "I get up—as if I am on autopilot. I head straight to the kitchen, and I can't fall back to sleep unless I put something into my mouth. My sister's son is staying with us for the summer, and I'm really embarrassed because I've been eating all of his snacks, and they are gone already!" Others have told us that their children have to hide their favorite foods in their rooms at night so that their parent with NES can't eat them. This worked some of the time, but there were some nights when the compulsion to eat a specific snack was so strong that the NES sufferer would enter the child's room and find the snack before the night was over.

No one likes to be caught eating in secret, and parents particularly don't like taking food away from their children in order to satisfy themselves. This driven, nighttime behavior is probably quite different from your usual daytime behavior, which demonstrates unclouded, or at least less clouded, judgment. When you are scolded by your children or your partner about your secretive eating, you probably feel embarrassed, which, in turn, lowers your self-esteem. This creates a cycle of negative feelings, like the others discussed above.

Exercise: Examining Your Thoughts

For this exercise, we ask you really to examine what thoughts you have about your eating at night. Do you worry about your loss of control? Do you personalize your eating behaviors and think that you are a bad person because of them? What other thoughts come to your mind when you think about your night eating?

In your journal, write down all of the ideas that you have about your night eating patterns. Later on, we will return to what you have written and will help you find out what your specific concerns are, so that eventually you will be able to change some of these distressing thoughts and feelings. (See chapters 8 and 9.)

Physical Activity

Physical activity or exercise provides many benefits, both physical and psychological. We all know that exercise can help to increase your endurance, lose weight, decrease your risk for cardiovascular disease, and make you stronger and more agile. What is not as well-known is the fact that exercise also provides a psychological boost by activating the release of certain chemicals in your body.

Endorphins

Endorphins are produced by exercise. They were named from the fusion of two words: "endogenous" (growing or produced inside) and "morphine" (a painkiller or sedative). When you exercise, endorphins are released in your brain and your nervous system. These peptides are your body's natural way of making itself feel good; they are responsible for what has been called the *runner's high*. Endorphins also help your body to increase your pain threshold.

Phenylethylamine

The body produces a natural stimulant called *phenylethylamine*, or PEA. This stimulant is chemically related to amphetamines ("speed"), but it is shorter-acting than these dangerous street drugs. PEA seems to have an even stronger effect on mood than endorphins do, although research on it is at an early stage.

Phenylethylamine usually decreases in people who are depressed. One British research team tested the effect of exercise on PEA levels and found that moderate exercise (defined as running for thirty minutes on a treadmill) raised PEA levels one day after the exercise was completed (Szabo, Billett, and Turner 2001).

This suggests that PEA is part of the physical benefit of exercise, and the authors of that study recommend including exercise as part of a treatment for depression.

This Chapter's Goals

- Exercise at least three times this week. Start with walking if you have not been exercising. Otherwise, pick your favorite physical activities to meet your exercise goals.

- Examine your thoughts about your night eating and write them down. On a daily or weekly basis, add to these thoughts, and save them for the exercises in part III.

- Consult a mental health professional or your physician if any of the disorders discussed in this chapter concern you.

CHAPTER 5

What Night Eating Syndrome Is Not

Although the patterns and emotions of NES may be very familiar to you, this syndrome is still relatively new to health care providers, as well as to the general public. Examined separately, the signs and symptoms of NES may look like other conditions. It is important for you to be aware of these other conditions, since you may be experiencing some of the problems caused by these other conditions together with NES. As you will see, some of the symptoms and stressors of these other conditions may even contribute to the problems you are having with NES.

Eating Disorders

You have probably seen television news stories or read newspaper or magazine articles on other eating disorders, such as anorexia, bulimia, and binge-eating disorder. These conditions receive more publicity than NES does because they were more clearly defined as conditions a lot longer. *Anorexia nervosa*, for example, was described at the end of the seventeenth century, and generations of doctors have been raised on the description of the emaciated, skeleton-like woman reported by the physician Richard Morton (1694). It was formally recognized as a disease in both Paris and London in 1874 at almost the same time.

For more than 100 years, doctors have struggled to help patients with anorexia nervosa, and the disorder has had the attention of the lay public for many years. Hardly a month goes by without a national magazine running a story about the curious behavior of young women who starve themselves. In this chapter, we consider anorexia and other eating disorders and compare them to NES.

Anorexia Nervosa

Anorexia nervosa is a very serious eating disorder that affects mostly women. Men account for only 10 percent of the population with the disorder. The core features of anorexia nervosa include (1) very restricted dieting, which results in (2) very low body weight together with (3) an unusual or exaggerated fear of being fat. All people with anorexia limit what they eat very strictly, and most also have a greatly increased level of physical activity, which accounts for their painful thinness.

Anorexia nervosa patients refuse to maintain a healthy weight for their height. As shown in the appendix, a body mass index (BMI) of less than 18.5 is considered underweight. Anorexics have BMIs of 17.5 or lower (for example, a 5 foot 4 woman weighing 100 pounds); some have BMIs as low as 14.5 (for example, a woman weighing 85 pounds at 5 foot 4). At weights in this range, women stop menstruating, and are at risk for osteoporosis, and men do not produce testosterone, their primary sex hormone. Anorexic men and women put themselves at risk for several health problems that often result from dehydration.

In addition to restricting their food intake, some patients with anorexia nervosa periodically break into eating binges, during which they lose control and eat large amounts of food in a very short period of time. This is called *anorexia nervosa, binge/ purge type*. After bingeing, overcome with guilt, some of these anorexics try to compensate by vomiting, taking laxatives, fasting, or exercising to the point of physical exhaustion. When bingeing and purging are not involved, the condition is called *anorexia nervosa, restricting type*.

When you do not eat proper nutrients and you purge by vomiting or using laxatives, you become severely dehydrated and you lose potassium. This loss results in an imbalance of electrolytes called *hypokalemia,* which can cause cardiac arrhythmias and eventual heart attacks. This is the most common cause of death among people with anorexia. Loss of strength and endurance, along with difficulties concentrating, also result from the severe malnutrition associated with anorexia. About a third of those who are extremely underweight develop *lanugo*, a fine, downy hair that may cover the face and body. This fine covering of hair usually occurs in newborns, but it also appears in anorexia, along with dry skin and brittle nails.

Some people with NES also have had anorexia nervosa in the past. While we do not know a great deal about this link, we do know that, occasionally, there are people who begin night eating while suffering from anorexia nervosa. Or, sometimes, during the stressful period when anorexia begins to improve, symptoms of NES may occur. Clearly, the relationship between NES and anorexia needs further research.

Bulimia Nervosa

Bulimia nervosa is commonly known as the disorder in which patients binge and then purge. Unlike patients classified as having anorexia nervosa, binge/purge type, those suffering from bulimia nervosa are not seriously underweight. Bulimia nervosa affects mostly women, but men are more frequently affected than is the case with anorexia nervosa. As with anorexia nervosa, people with bulimia nervosa are overly influenced by their perceptions of their body weight and shape. Unlike patients with anorexia nervosa, who deny that they ever feel hungry, those with bulimia nervosa freely acknowledge their preoccupation with thoughts of food. Because women with bulimia nervosa are not as severely underweight as those with anorexia nervosa, as a rule they do not lose their menstrual cycles and, similarly, men's testosterone levels do not significantly decrease.

Two distinctive signs of bulimia nervosa stand out. One is the swelling of the salivary glands in a bulimic's cheeks, which makes them look a little bit like a chipmunk's. The swelling is due to the glands becoming irritated from the extremely acid stomach contents brought up during vomiting. This acid is also responsible for dissolving the enamel of the teeth, with resulting tooth decay that is seen even in very young bulimics. The other distinctive feature of bulimia nervosa is the scarred fingers and knuckles of bulimic patients that result from their being used to stimulate vomiting. These distinctive scars may be referred to clinically as *Russell's sign*.

Some of the complications of bulimia nervosa are more serious than the obvious ones just discussed. Some bulimics abuse laxatives in their efforts to prevent the absorption of food they consumed in their binge eating. Chronic bowel disorders can be caused by the laxative abuse. Another complication of bulimia nervosa, rare but life threatening, is the rupturing of the stomach caused by the large amounts of food that are consumed during a binge. Finally, as in anorexia nervosa described above, the often chaotic bingeing, vomiting, and laxative abuse can lead to serious electrolyte disturbances that may affect the heart, up to and including death from cardiac arrest.

Once again, we know very little about any clear relationship between NES and bulimia nervosa. Very rare case reports in the past suggest that it is possible for a person to sufferer from both disorders (Gupta 1991; Williamson et al. 1989). Because these reports were written before their authors were aware of NES, whether or not bulimia nervosa and NES occurred in the same person during the same time period is unclear.

Binge-Eating Disorder

Binge-eating disorder (BED) consists of eating very large amounts of food in a hurried and ashamed manner. These binges take place along with feeling a loss of control, as if you cannot stop yourself from eating, and as if all of the available food must be consumed before you can stop eating. Binge-eating disorder differs from bulimia nervosa because it does not involve purging by vomiting or by laxative abuse. Therefore, most people with BED, more than half of whom are women, are overweight or even severely obese.

Binge-eating disorder coexists with NES more often than with either anorexia or bulimia. Perhaps this is so because so many people with NES are overweight, as are most of those with BED. Among people seeking treatment for weight loss or help with their eating problems, it has been reported that as many as 10 to 15 percent of those with BED also have NES (Adami, Meneghelli, and Scopinaro 1999; Powers et al. 1999).

Even though they may occur together, there are important differences between BED and NES. First, the typical amount that a night eater consumes at one sitting during the night is much more like a snack than a meal: on average, between 200 and 400 calories is consumed. This amount is much less than the caloric intake of a binge that might be eaten by a person with BED, which can add up to 2000, 3000, or even more calories. A second difference between NES and BED is that, as a general rule, binges do not take place during the night, in sharp distinction to the regular nighttime eating of a night eater. The third difference is the presence of a serious sleep disorder in persons with NES, demonstrated by their frequent awakenings. Sleep disturbance is not a usual feature of BED.

Exercise: Do You Have Binge-Eating Disorder?

To determine whether you may have a problem with BED, ask yourself the following questions:

Do you

- frequently eat *large* quantities of food in short periods of time, often secretly, without regard to feelings of hunger or fullness?

- feel out of control during binges?

- eat large quantities of food rapidly, without really tasting the food?

- eat alone?

- feel shame, disgust, or guilt after a binge?

If you answered yes to the first two questions, and to one or more of the last three questions, you may have BED in addition to NES. If so, you will want to pay close attention to chapter 2 and to all the chapters in part III. These chapters emphasize regulating your food intake and provide help for changing the thinking and behaviors that are related to both binge eating and night eating.

Sleep Disorders

Sleep disorders in general have been less publicized than eating disorders. Yet, if you have a problem with your sleeping pattern, you know that they are no less troubling. You have probably heard a lot about insomnia, the most prevalent sleep disorder. However, there are several other problems that may plague people at night, problems such as sleep apnea, delayed sleep phase disorder, periodic leg movements, and restless legs syndrome. These will be described below, but first let's examine the disorder most similar to NES, nocturnal sleep-related eating disorder, or NS-RED.

Nocturnal Sleep-Related Eating Disorder (NS-RED)

People suffering from NS-RED eat at night, as do those with NES. The major distinction between the two disorders is how conscious you are of your eating. People with NS-RED are largely unconscious when they eat; they may actually be sleepwalking at the time. In addition, in the morning after night eating, they usually have no memory of having eaten the night before. These are the people who report awakening in the morning to find wrappers or crumbs in their beds, or food still on their hands or in their hair. Furthermore, persons with NS-RED may eat unusual or even nonfood items at night. They report having eaten such things as buttered cigarettes, salt or sugar sandwiches, or frozen, raw, or spoiled foods (Schenck and Mahowald 1994).

People with NS-RED are more likely to injure themselves at night by either cutting or burning themselves while preparing foods, or even by bumping into walls and furniture. In striking contrast to the limited consciousness demonstrated by those with NS-RED, people with NES are usually fully conscious of their choice to eat, although they may have occasional episodes of eating without having much recollection. The table below compares the characteristics of NES and NS-RED.

NES versus NS-RED		
Characteristic	**NES**	**NS-RED**
Consciousness	Yes	No
Amnesia about their night eating	No	Yes
Associated sleepwalking	No	Yes
Eats nonfoods or unusual foods	No	Yes
Depressed mood	Yes	No
Evening overeating	Yes	No

Sleep Apnea

In Greek, *apnea* literally means "without breath." If you have sleep apnea, basically, you may stop and start breathing several hundred times per night. There are three types of sleep apnea (the latter two types are the most common):

1. *Central sleep apnea* occurs when the brain fails to signal the body to breathe.

2. *Obstructive sleep apnea* is caused by a blockage of soft tissue near the back of the throat that collapses and closes off the windpipe during sleep.

3. *Mixed sleep apnea* is a combination of the other two types of apnea.

If you have sleep apnea, usually you will be without breath for more than ten seconds many times every hour, before your brain will arouse you from sleep to breathe again. Each time you stop breathing, it is called an *apnea event*.

Snoring is one of the signs of sleep apnea. Sleep apnea affects more than twelve million Americans. Its risk factors include being male, overweight, and over forty, but anyone can have problems with sleep apnea. Unlike NES, where you awaken from sleep and get up to eat, sleep apnea causes your brain simply to arouse your body to trigger breathing again. Sometimes you will awaken, but most often you will fall back to sleep, and the next day you will not recall your fitful night's sleep.

When you have NES, you may feel tired during the day from having had problems falling and staying asleep. When you have sleep apnea, you will feel tired from your fitful sleep, but you also will feel tired from the reduced amount of oxygen in your body caused by your apnea events. Sleep apnea also can lead to other serious health problems like high blood pressure, heart attack, and even lung failure. Sleep apnea is quite different from NES, but the two can occur together.

If you have reason to think that you may have sleep apnea, it's important to be properly diagnosed because of its serious health consequences. There are very effective treatments for sleep apnea and, if you have it, you should get treatment without delay. Our own research with inpatient sleep studies has not linked NES and sleep apnea, but the night awakenings, association with obesity, and daytime sleepiness provide the potential for some people to experience both of these conditions together.

Exercise: Do You Have Sleep Apnea?

If you suspect that you suffer from sleep apnea, here are some signs to check (adapted from the American Sleep Apnea Association):

- Does your bed partner observe you choking, gasping, or holding your breath during sleep?

- Are you a loud, habitual snorer?

- Does someone else in your family, a brother, sister, parent, or grandparent, suffer from sleep apnea?

- Do you feel tired and groggy on awakening?

- Are you often sleepy during waking hours or can you fall asleep quickly?

- Are you overweight or do you have a large neck?

If you answered yes to any of these questions, you should discuss this issue with your doctor. Your snoring and grogginess may be related to sleep apnea or a related condition that may need observation or treatment.

Delayed Sleep Phase Syndrome

People who suffer from *delayed sleep phase syndrome* (DSPS) are often thought of as night owls. But, unlike those who prefer to be up at night, if you have DSPS, you have no control over the time you are asleep or awake. You simply cannot fall asleep earlier or get up earlier than your body will allow. Essentially, people who suffer from DSPS have problems with their internal time clocks, or circadian rhythms. (*Circadian rhythms* are biological characteristics or functions characterized by twenty-four-hour cycles.) Such people are flipped around. They can force themselves to wake up early, to conform to the typical workday and normal life activities. But this early wake-up call can cause daytime tiredness and disorientation, since the body and mind's sleep rhythm is opposite to that of most people whose circadian rhythms dictate that they sleep at night and be awake during the day.

If you do a lot of traveling across time zones, you may have experienced a temporary form of DSPS. This usually disappears after a few days of adjusting to the new time zone. For chronic DSPS, there are some treatments available that may help recover the normal circadian rhythm. These treatments include the use of melatonin and light therapy. Under the direction of a physician, these treatments may work to help those with DSPS readjust their sleep-wake cycles.

We are still not certain whether there is any association between NES and DSPS. It was once hypothesized that DSPS could contribute to the late night eating. This has not been confirmed or denied. Again, as with other eating and sleep disorders, you may have suffered from these other conditions as well as from NES in the past or currently.

Periodic Limb Movements

Have you ever felt yourself dozing off at night, only to be awakened by the sudden jerking of an arm or a leg? If so, you were experiencing a *periodic limb movement* (PLM). These jerks or twitches occur during light sleep, such as in stage 1 or stage 2 sleep that was discussed in chapter 3. Although everyone experiences a little jerkiness occasionally, if you suffer from PLM syndrome, these twitches will occur at least five times an hour. As with sleep apnea, PLM may first be recognized by a bed partner.

There is no apparent danger from these twitches, just as there is no definite cause. They can, however, cause you to wake up, and you may have problems falling back asleep. Treatments for the PLM syndrome exist, particularly medications that affect your central nervous system. To date, there has been no direct link shown between NES and PLM, although some research suggests that PLM may be linked to NS-RED (Schenck and Mahowald 1994).

Restless Leg Syndrome

Restless leg syndrome (RLS) is not simply a sleeping disorder; however, many people experience RLS problems while trying to fall asleep. If you have RLS, you have the urge to move or rub your legs frequently. This urge is stronger when your legs are still or at rest. This genetically inherited condition can become more frequent with extreme temperatures, excessive tiredness, and consumption of alcohol or caffeine. Similar to PLM, the cause of RLS is not well-defined, and it does not seem to be related to NES (Dinges et al., unpublished observations, 2003).

Mood Disorders

As you read in chapter 4, many night eaters feel depressed. You will remember that depression can occur with different intensities and with many different symptoms. Some people feel worse in the morning; others, especially night eaters, feel worse in the evening. Some people eat and sleep more than usual, others eat and sleep less. Some people are not able to get out of bed; others can still function, but they have difficulty concentrating or summoning the energy and interest to work or to go out with friends.

All of these symptoms are characteristic of depression. The disorder manifests in different ways in different people. Major depressive disorder differs from NES in some important ways. First, one of the symptoms of depression is early morning awakenings, where people wake up an hour or two before they are supposed to and they are unable to fall back to sleep. Most of the awakenings in people with NES occur during the first half of the night, so this represents an important distinction. Second, lack of appetite in the morning is not characteristic of major depressive disorder. Instead, appetite is usually lacking throughout the entire day, or the opposite, it is increased throughout the entire day. These two distinctions help to differentiate these two disorders.

With that said, many people who have NES also have had major depression at some point in their lives. If you suspect that you are depressed, and it is interfering with your ability to function throughout the day, you should consult a mental health professional or your physician. This is especially true if you have feelings of wanting to hurt yourself or someone else. If your depression does not interfere with your ability to function, continue reading the next section. Perhaps your depressed feelings are linked to your night eating and could be relieved, at least in part, by changes we will suggest that you make.

Do You Have One of These Disorders?

You have just read about some of the other disorders that may be similar or related to NES. Do you think that you may suffer from any of these? Some of you may have had other eating disorders in the past, and some of you may currently suffer from sleep disorders or mood disorders. To determine whether you have one of these disorders, ask yourself the following questions.

Exercise: Do You Have an Eating, Sleeping, or Mood Disorder?

- Do the symptoms described for any of these disorders seem to fit your own experience?

- Do those symptoms interfere with your ability to function, or do they cause you problems in your work or your relationships?

- Do those symptoms cause you any health problems?

- If you answered yes to any of these, you may want to consult your health care provider or a mental health specialist to see if you can obtain relief from the distress you are experiencing.

This Chapter's Goals

- Become familiar with the disorders described in this chapter.

- Identify whether any of these disorders fits your own experience, and talk to your health care provider or mental health professional about them in order to obtain relief.

PART II

The Biology of
Night Eating

Chapters 6 and 7 will introduce you to the research that has begun to focus on the underlying biological mechanisms of NES. Scientific study of NES is still in its early stages, but what is known about genetics and the role of hormones is explained.

CHAPTER 6

It's a Family Affair: The Genetics of Night Eating Syndrome

You may feel that your night eating is a personal problem that none of your friends and family can ever understand. Yet, you may be surprised to learn that recent research suggests that NES runs in families. This condition may actually be inherited. What does this mean for you?

A Brief History of Genetics

Before you can understand how NES may be passed from a parent to a child, let's refresh your understanding of the science of genetics. Early attempts to figure out the role of heredity in humans include reports from about 500 A.D. in the authoritative book of Jewish tradition, the *Talmud*. There is a description in the Talmud of the bleeding disorder, hemophilia, which, it was noted, ran in families. Despite this and other rare examples, most of what was known about human heredity was highly speculative until recent times.

Mendel = genetics = 1866 PEAS & lover

An Eye for an Eye; A Pea for a Pea

A basic understanding of heredity remained elusive until 1866, when the studies of the Moravian monk, Gregor Mendel, were published. That publication ushered in our modern understanding of genetics. Yet, at the time, his research attracted little or no attention, because it seemed far removed from practical applications to human disease. Why was there such lack of interest? Perhaps because Mendel's study participants were garden peas.

Although Mendel's research was with plants, the basic underlying principles of heredity that he discovered also apply to people and other animals because the mechanisms of heredity are essentially the same for all complex life forms. You may have a vague recollection of this research from your high school freshman biology course.

Among Mendel's key findings was the discovery of the laws governing the color of peas produced by crossing peas of two different colors. He demonstrated that the color of the peas resulting from crossing yellow peas with green peas was not an in-between shade, as you might expect. Instead, all of the first generation of these crosses were of the same color, yellow. Then, when he crossed the second generation yellow peas with each other, Mendel discovered that the original green reappeared in some of the peas of the third generation.

Eventually, this result led to our current knowledge of dominant and recessive genes. Mendel explained his findings by proposing that yellow was the dominant color, while green was recessive. He proposed the theory that each individual pea possesses two *factors* that determine a specific characteristic such as color, and that each parent transmits only one of these two factors to any particular offspring. It took many years before the significance of these factors became known. But they are recognized today as *genes*, the agents responsible for the transmission of all heritable characteristics from parents to children.

Think of these findings in terms of human eye color. As with the yellow peas, the gene for brown eyes is dominant. Say, for example, your mother has brown eyes, and your father blue. Your mother may have either two dominant genes (two brown genes), or she may have one dominant and one recessive (a brown and a blue). Your father, having blue eyes, has two recessive genes. If your mother has two dominant genes, you will have brown eyes since her gene will be dominant over the recessive gene from your father. If your mother has one dominant and one recessive gene, you have a fifty-fifty chance of having brown eyes. If your mother passes her dominant gene on to you, you will have brown eyes. If your mother passes her recessive gene on to you, when it is crossed with the recessive gene your father passed on to you, you will have blue eyes.

Human Genetics

Understanding human heredity began in Great Britain about the same time that Mendel was studying peas in Moravia (now in the Czech Republic). These efforts were led by Frances Galton, a cousin of Charles Darwin, who studied the hereditary transmission of abilities within families. Perhaps motivated by the evident intelligence within his own family, Galton conducted a systematic study of the biographies of prominent Englishmen. He clearly demonstrated that both intelligence and physical stature were transmitted within families. He also introduced the study of twins and performed the first studies of the critical gene-by-environment interactions, which we will discuss below. He proposed that, since identical twins are genetically identical, any differences between them must be due to environmental influences, and he tried to measure these differences.

In 1953, Watson and Crick discovered the basic structure of genetic material, and how it affects the characteristics of all living beings. They showed that genes are complex chemical structures, arranged in the form of a double helix, each of which contains all of the genetic information that is necessary to construct all the parts of organisms that range from simple fruit flies to complex mammals like human beings. This breakthrough discovery led to an enormous amount of research that has solved some of the traditional problems of medicine and has uncovered many new ones.

Some important fruits of this research have been to identify specific problems within a gene that give rise to disorders produced by single genes. There are a vast number of such genes and such disorders, and some progress has been made in understanding the defects in some single genes that lead to disease. But as we learn more about these problems, it has also become apparent that disorders due to defects in single genes are rare and cause only a very small fraction of human illnesses. Our understanding of obesity is a case in point.

The Genetics of Obesity

It had long been believed that a single gene was responsible for a rare form of severe obesity in certain mice, called "ob/ob mice." Years of study eventually led to the discovery of the chemical structure of the ob/ob gene, which codes for—or programs—a substance, *leptin*, that helps to control the fat content of the body. Researchers found that the ob/ob mouse's obesity was due to a defect in the ob/ob gene that made it unable to produce leptin. (See chapter 7 for a discussion of leptin and its unusual patterns in night eaters.)

The discovery of leptin led to the hope that human obesity might be due to a defect in a single gene, for example, in the ob/ob gene, and that such a defect could be countered by administrating leptin. This hope was realized, but only in part. Leptin did cure the obesity of the very rare humans (babies) who had inherited the defective ob/ob gene. But, almost none of the 70 million Americans with obesity have this defective gene, and so have received no benefit from leptin.

Genes and the Environment

Does the fact that a defective ob/ob gene is only a very rare cause of human obesity mean that genetics plays almost no role in obesity? The answer is no. The study of twins introduced by Galton 150 years ago helped scientists to estimate the extent of genetic influences on a wide variety of human diseases. Among these conditions, obesity probably has one of the largest genetic contributions. When Swedish twins who were separated at birth, and thus had no environmental influences in common, were studied, it was estimated that 70 percent of their body weight was genetically determined (Stunkard et al. 1990).

Obesity and overweight are rapidly increasing in the American population and now affect 65 percent of the adult population (Flegal et al. 2002), so detecting and countering the contributing genetic factors is an important challenge. Yet, you must be well aware that heredity is not the only factor that causes obesity. In many health conditions, genes are only one part of the cause. The other is environment, which brings us to the idea of *gene-by-environment interactions.*

Genes completely determine the color of eyes and hair. The environment has no effect, and thus for hair and eye color there is no gene-by-environment interaction. Heredity, however, does not completely determine human behavior; the environment also exerts an important influence. The 70 percent genetic influence on body weight means only that some people are very vulnerable to becoming obese. They, like you, do not become obese in a vacuum, however.

As detailed in chapter 2, to become obese, you must consume more calories than you expend. If you do not have a genetic vulnerability to obesity, it is likely that you will not overeat and become obese. The converse, of course, is also true. If you do have a genetic vulnerability, it is more likely that you will overeat and become obese.

All human behavior is determined by this interaction between genes and environment. This gene-by-environment interaction is as true of night eating syndrome as of obesity or any of the behavioral disorders that afflict us. Given this understanding, let us turn to what we have learned about genetic influences on NES.

NES and Genetics

During the course of our studies of NES we have made it a point to ask night eaters whether any other members of their families suffer from the disorder. We've been particularly interested in first-degree family members, those who share the most genetic similarities: parents, siblings, and children. We found that 17 percent of all first-degree relatives of NES patients were affected, while only 5 percent of first-degree family members of the controls were affected. The frequency of NES among family members of those with the disorder is as great as that of diseases with known genetic backgrounds, and far higher than for people without NES.

Figures 6.1 and 6.2 illustrate the genetic basis of NES through the family trees of two night eaters. The first family tree shows that three siblings have NES, as did their father, who is deceased. The second family tree shows that one member of each of the three generations has, or had, NES.

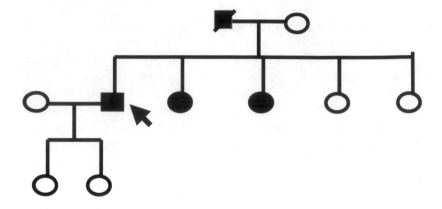

Figure 6.1: A family with an extensive genetic influence of NES. Notes: Squares indicate males and circles indicate females. Solid-color males and females have NES. No color (or clear) males and females do not have NES. Diagonal lines through family members indicate they are deceased. The arrow points to the family member who actively participated in the study.

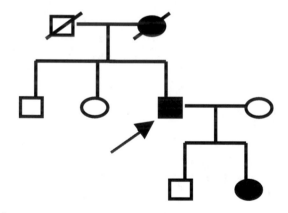

Figure 6.2: A family tree with three generations of NES sufferers.

What does the influence of heredity on the night eating syndrome mean for you? Is it a reason for discouragement and despair? Not at all. As noted above, a genetic influence on the color of one's eyes or hair is absolute. But that is not at all the case with genetic influences on human behavior. Whether you develop a behavior depends to a great extent on the environment in which you were raised, and in which you are living at the present time.

Gene-by-Environment Interactions

We know from the number of family members with NES that there are very strong genetic influences on NES, just as there are for obesity. Yet even if you are genetically susceptible to obesity, it does not mean that you will become obese. If you are obese, it also does not mean that you will remain obese. As stated above, environmental influences also play an important role.

Social class is one very strong environmental influence on obesity. People from the upper social classes are far less likely to be obese than people from the lower social classes. The reasons for this environmental influence are not fully understood, but they are probably related to lifestyles.

Higher up the social scale, people tend to eat less food in terms of quantity and less fatty food in terms of quality, and they often have more access to fresher, healthier food. They also may be more likely to participate in physical activities. For example, parks and recreational areas are safer and better maintained in higher income areas than in lower income ones. Restaurants in well-to-do areas tend to serve smaller portions than do the fast food restaurants that are often the mainstay of families in poorer neighborhoods. And for those in the upper class who do become obese, treatment is far more highly regarded, and available.

We are just beginning to understand the environmental influences that may foster night eating among vulnerable people, and we are even further from understanding how to control it. We do know, however, that stressful environments can provide the stimulus for night eating in those who are genetically vulnerable; that is, a stressful environment can trigger the onset of NES and can help to maintain it. In the following chapters you will find approaches to understanding how night eating syndrome comes about and ways to cope with it. Progress is being made and help is on the way.

Who Else Has NES?

You probably know that night eating syndrome is not well recognized in the general population, and you, like most night eaters, may not understand how your genetic background can provide the basis for the development of NES. Have your genes played a role in your NES? Talk to your family, your parents and siblings, your children, and nephews and nieces. Do any of them report any indications of night eating? Do you recall any behaviors that you now understand might indicate that they suffer from NES?

As shown in figures 6.1 and 6.2, there are families in which more than one person is a night eater; and the more we learn about the condition, the more families we find with multiple sufferers. If you have a family member who is a night eater, or two or three family members with the condition, you may now better understand your reasons for developing NES. Your habits and the feeling of being out of control are not your fault—you may have been programmed to experience these difficulties.

Exercise: Find Others Who Have NES

Although you need to aim at taking control, it could be that your family's heredity predisposed you, or put you at higher risk, for developing NES. Understanding how much genetic pressure drives you to this behavior could help give you some insight and cause you to feel less responsible for your night eating.

1. Go out and find other people who suffer from this problem.

2. Get in touch with all the members of your immediate and distant family.

3. Interview them about their eating habits.

4. You may be surprised to find that there are others like you in your family.

5. And, even if no one in your family has NES, interview everyone you know who is overweight. You may be surprised to discover there are many others like you.

As one night eater told us, "Finding out that there were other people like me made me feel much better about myself. It made me feel like I wasn't a freak."

This Chapter's Goals

- Investigate whether any of your family members, either living or deceased, suffer(ed) from NES. If you find any, ask them how it affects their lives now, or how it affected their lives previously, and what helped them.

- Whether you are overweight or normal weight, look to your family again, both living and deceased, to see if there are gene-by-environment interactions present that may have influenced your weight. Look for factors such as a generational history of overweight or a tradition of frying many of your foods.

CHAPTER 7

Hormones

It is clear that NES is not a simple condition. You have already learned a lot about the sleeping, eating, and mood-related problems that contribute to your difficulties with NES. Now we will deal with hormones. If you are a woman, the word "hormone" will immediately bring to mind estrogen and progesterone, hormone replacement therapy, and menopause. If you are a man, your thoughts may turn toward testosterone. These are the more familiar hormones that our bodies produce.

Hormones are essentially chemicals produced in one of the *endocrine glands* (for example, the pituitary, ovaries, testes, and thyroid glands) that are sent to target cells in the body to help regulate various bodily functions. Scientists in this field have learned that your hormones play a key role in NES. An imbalance of hormones related to your sleep and stress levels may be affecting both your eating and sleeping patterns. There are a number of hormones that that are currently being linked to NES, including the stress hormones, cortisol and ACTH; the sleep-regulating hormone melatonin; and the appetite-regulating hormones, leptin and ghrelin. In this chapter you will learn more about these hormones, as well as about glucose and insulin, which help to regulate your eating and your metabolism.

Your Body's Response to Stress

Many people report that their night eating began during a period of stress. You may even be able to recall the specific stressful event (or events) that triggered your own night eating. You may also be aware that stress can wreak havoc not only with your emotions but also with your health. The good news is that today we understand a great deal about stress and how the body responds to it, and we are learning more every day. We want to help you realize that stress is much more than just the feeling of being tense and under pressure. There is an entire section of your nervous system and a number of hormones that respond when you are under stress. These responses can cause physiological problems beyond just feeling anxious and stressed out.

The HPA Axis

The system that responds to stress has the daunting title of the *hypothalamic-pituitary-adrenal (HPA) axis*, referring to the three interacting systems of: the *hypothalamus*, the *pituitary gland*, and the *adrenal glands*. As you will see, the HPA axis governs many of the chemical responses in your body that help you respond to and cope with stress.

Excess stimulation of the HPA axis, that is, being under constant stress, has been linked with a number of common physical ailments, including obesity and memory disturbance (Raber 1998), depression (Kennedy et al. 1989), insomnia (Hajak et al. 1995), fibromyalgia (Adler et al. 1999) and chronic fatigue syndrome (Kuratsune et al. 1998).

Activity of the HPA axis triggered by stress contributes to the depositing of fat inside the abdominal walls, a particularly dangerous condition that is marked by large waistlines. One pathway to abdominal obesity is experiencing chronic, ongoing stress (Ljung et al. 2000). The abdomen is the most dangerous place to have excess fat, as it has been linked both to the development of type II diabetes and cardiovascular disease.

The Release of Hormones

You may be curious how the HPA axis works and how the balance and dance of the various glands and secretions work together either to promote emotional and physical health or to burden the body with illness. Learning more about the hormonal release process will help you reach a better understanding of the effects of stress on your night eating.

Corticotropic-Releasing Hormone (CRH)

When you come under stress, your cognitive brain processes (i.e., your thoughts) stimulate processes that produce your emotions. This response to stress then involves the *hypothalamus*, a small structure deep in the brain that governs many bodily functions. The hypothalamus secretes a powerful hormone, known as the *corticotropic-releasing hormone* (CRH). This hormone, in turn, activates the pituitary gland, the master gland, located at the base of the brain. The CRH tells the pituitary gland to release the *adrenocorticotropic hormone* (ACTH). What does ACTH do?

ACTH and Cortisol

Adrenocorticotropic hormone (ACTH) is a stress hormone. It stimulates the production of yet another stress hormone, *cortisol*, by the adrenal glands, which are located atop of both of the kidneys. Cortisol is essential in aiding the body to cope during times of stress in many ways. It helps to regulate blood pressure and other cardiovascular responses to stressful situations. It also helps to regulate how the body uses fats, carbohydrates, and proteins. Without a proper cortisol response, your body will not be able to function efficiently and you will not be able to keep up with the daily challenges of life.

Unlike ACTH, which is released in irregular bursts throughout the day, cortisol has a steadier pattern, often coinciding with human wake and sleep cycles. Cortisol levels rise very early in the morning and fall throughout the rest of the day. In persons in whom this rhythm is disturbed, there also may be disturbances in mineral balance, control of blood sugar, and, as you might suspect, responses to stress. Although a lack of cortisol is associated with fatigue, allergies, and arthritis, too much cortisol can also have a negative effect on the body.

Short-term elevations, or bursts, of cortisol are important for dealing with unexpected life events, such as the sudden death of a loved one, a car accident, getting fired, or even for recovering from an illness. However, chronically elevated levels of cortisol are harmful to your health, having both a physical and psychological impact. You may feel tired and depressed, and signs of aging may speed up with loss of muscle mass and thinning of bones. Excess stimulation of the HPA axis plays a significant role in the origins of obesity and diabetes. Overproduction of both ACTH and cortisol will stress the body and eventually lead it to a state of exhaustion and illness.

Recent research has shown that people who suffer from NES have higher levels of ACTH and cortisol throughout the twenty-four hours of the day. Interestingly, in two studies, the production of cortisol in the night eaters showed the usual circadian (twenty-four hour) pattern of higher levels in the early morning, falling during the course of the day (Allison et al., Working paper 2003; Birketvedt et al. 1999), indicating that this hormonal pattern, although elevated, is not shifted, as is the eating cycle in NES.

Two studies measured different aspects of cortisol. One examined participants in the hospital using frequent blood samples (Birketvedt et al. 1999). The second examined participants at home using samples of saliva (Allison et al., Working paper 2003). Both studies showed that the elevated cortisol levels in NES occur consistently, whether collected by blood or saliva and whether in a hospital environment or in the home. These measures of hormonal differences between those with and without NES demonstrate that the stress you feel is not just in your mind; it is also playing a critical role in the functioning of your HPA axis.

The hormonal effects of stress can trigger overeating. Two ingenious studies demonstrated this. One study invited a group of women into a laboratory where they performed a stressful task (Epel et al. 2000). After completing the task, they were left in a room with a variety of snacks. The women who reacted more severely to the stressful event, and whose levels of cortisol were higher, ate more food, especially sweet food, than the women who did not react as strongly. It seems likely that your cravings for food at such an unusual time—the night—are linked to your experience of stress. However, we are still putting together all of the pieces of the complicated puzzle we call the human body.

The second study, completed recently in Norway, has shown the long-term adverse effects of chronic overstimulation of the HPA axis (Birketvedt et al. 2002). This study compared the responses of women with and without NES who were matched for age and weight. A dose of CRH, the hormonal go-between the brain centers in the hypothalamus and the pituitary gland, was administered to these women, and their concentrations of ACTH and cortisol were measured. Striking differences were found. The night eaters showed far less production of ACTH and cortisol in response to the CRH injection than did the control subjects. What does this mean?

As noted above, the usual function of CRH is to trigger the release of ACTH and cortisol. In the Norwegian study, those who were not night eaters showed this expected response. However, the failure of the night eaters to respond in this usual manner suggests that they have a defect in their HPA axis. The most likely cause of this defect is exhaustion of the HPA axis; it has begun to wear out as a result of overstimulation during long periods of time. This explanation seems particularly likely, given the consistently elevated levels of ACTH and cortisol that we, and others, have found among night eaters. Again, these ill effects of long-term HPA axis overstimulation have been reported to occur in different disorders, ranging from obesity to memory defects (Raber 1998).

Melatonin—A Sleep Hormone

Similar to the hormonal responses to stress, there is an intricate rhythm created by hormones that help you to sleep. The primary sleep-related hormone, and one that you may be familiar with, is melatonin. *Melatonin* helps the body to know when it's time to sleep by using light cues. During the daytime, light activates the optic nerves which suppresses the production of melatonin. In the dark, when the optic nerve is no longer active, melatonin is produced, accompanying sleep and perhaps promoting sleep. The level of melatonin usually increases in the late evening, along with your sleepiness, and continues increasing until about midnight. After that time it begins to decrease, as your body starts waking up. People with the highest blood levels of melatonin sleep most soundly.

Disturbances in melatonin production are associated with some well-known conditions. Have you ever traveled across time zones and had difficulty adjusting to the time change, also known as jet lag? *Jet lag* is the interruption of your normal biological rhythms. Do you work a night shift job? You may be altering your melatonin production artificially not only by changing your sleeping pattern, but also by decreasing your exposure to daylight during the daytime, when you are trying to catch up on your sleep. A reduced release of melatonin also has been associated with difficulty sleeping and/or staying asleep.

Your doctor may recommend using a melatonin supplement for difficulty falling asleep or staying asleep. These supplements can be purchased over the counter, but usually in higher doses than those recommended by experts in the field (personal communication with Dr. R. Wurtman at the Massachusetts Institute of Technology). The optimal dose is a mere 0.3 mg, while the average over-the-counter supplement is larger.

Research on melatonin in NES sufferers is still in its early stages. The first study to examine melatonin in night eaters reported that levels of this hormone did *not* increase in night eaters at night, as it should and as it did among non–night eaters (Birketvedt et al. 1999). On the other hand, a more recent study of night eaters failed to confirm the inhibition of the rise of melatonin at night (Allison et al., Unpublished observations). You can see that we are still a long way from unraveling the complex story of melatonin.

Hormones Related to Eating

We have already addressed some of the hormonal influences on two of the three primary disorders involved in night eating: emotions and sleeping. There are also hormones that are related to your eating habits. Leptin and ghrelin are two hormones linked to the regulation of eating in humans.

Leptin

Leptin is produced by fat tissue and secreted into the bloodstream, where it travels to the brain and other tissues, decreasing one's appetite. The amount of leptin in the system depends upon the amount of fat stored in the body. Thus, leptin levels are higher in overweight and obese persons. The word "leptin" originates from the Greek word *leptos*, meaning "thin." If you are overweight or obese, the higher levels of leptin may prevent you from becoming even more overweight. When the fat stored in the body is depleted, such as during times of famine or in the presence of anorexia nervosa, leptin levels are low. This depletion of leptin is a cue for the body to consume more food.

There may also be a relationship between leptin and sleep. Sleep deprivation seems to reduce leptin, which signals to the body that it is underfed. This faulty cue, if continued over a long period of time, might result in your metabolism slowing down, an increase in your fat deposits, and an increase in your appetite.

regulate sleep for better metabolism

Leptin rises at night, as does melatonin, and tends to keep your hunger under control while you are sleeping. A hormone study of NES found that leptin did not rise at night in night eaters, as it does in most people (Birketvedt et al. 1999). This finding suggests that leptin may not be suppressing your hunger while you are sleeping. However, as in the more recent research on melatonin, this absence of a rise in leptin at night has not been confirmed. As is the case with melatonin, more research is needed (Allison et al., Unpublished observations).

Ghrelin

The effects of *ghrelin* have been described only recently. It is produced in the stomach and released before you eat, and is believed to be a trigger to start eating. Unfortunately, when you are dieting ghrelin levels rise, which increases your appetite and, after a while, makes it difficult for you to continue losing weight. This may be part of the reason that the human body is so resistant to maintaining significant weight losses.

One important observation has been the response of ghrelin to gastric bypass surgery for the treatment of very severe obesity. After this surgery, the production of ghrelin in the stomach is sharply reduced. The author of an important study of ghrelin, Dr. David Cummings, has proposed that the reduction in hunger following bypass surgery is the reason why people lose weight so easily and with so little distress, while people who lose weight using many of the current diets must constantly deal with feelings of hunger (Cummings et al. 2002).

Identifying the genes that are regulated by leptin and ghrelin will improve our knowledge of how these hormones affect weight and appetite, and may also offer new targets for drugs designed to stimulate weight loss. However, the Food and Drug Administration (FDA) has not yet approved these hormones for regular supplemental use by humans.

Regulating Blood Sugar: Glucose and Insulin

Some inquisitive night eaters have wondered if their glucose levels are lower than usual during the night, which would potentially trigger their midnight hunger. Glucose is a simple sugar that is the body's main energy source. The body metabolizes glucose to unleash this energy. Insulin, which is produced in the pancreas, controls the rate of glucose metabolism. If you are insulin-resistant, your body's cells do not allow insulin to metabolize the glucose, and higher levels of insulin result. The inability of insulin to process glucose is the underlying cause of type II diabetes.

One study (Birketvedt et al. 1999) restricted food intake of both night eaters and controls to four small meals—each about 400 calories—at 8:00 A.M., 12:00 P.M., 4:00 P.M., and 8:00 P.M. Apparently, when under tight control of their food intake, night eaters did not exhibit abnormalities in their glucose and insulin levels. It's not surprising that during this study the levels of glucose and insulin did not differ between the night eaters and controls. As you well know, this structured meal schedule is not the way night eaters actually eat.

To see how night eaters respond to their usual disturbed food intake, we performed a study in which food intake was not restricted (Allison et al., Unpublished observations). Instead, participants were encouraged to bring their favorite snacks to the hospital. They were provided food upon request throughout the day, and there was a snack tray at their bedside throughout the evening and night. Dr. Rexford Ahima, an endocrinologist at the University of Pennsylvania, found that this more natural food schedule produced a far different pattern of glucose and insulin than did the tightly controlled diet used in the first study.

This time we found that glucose was somewhat higher in night eaters across the twenty-four-hour day, possibly implying early impairment of glucose utilization in this group. Eating according to their usual pattern also resulted in higher levels of insulin in the control subjects during the day, and higher levels of insulin in the night eaters during the night.

These two studies suggest that when people are forced to eat on a regular schedule, glucose and insulin can be kept at normal levels—even among night eaters. However, when eating as they usually do, night eaters show marked differences in these important regulators from the subjects who were acting as controls, a difference that could imply more serious problems for them in the future. This important finding adds a strong emphasis to the recommendation that night eaters should make an effort to create a regular eating schedule during the day, as outlined in chapter 2.

This Chapter's Goals

- Become familiar with the hormones linked to NES.

- Stay informed about news items that mention these hormones to make yourself more knowledgeable about the progress being made in researching this promising area.

Glucose: body's main energy source

Pancreas
  ∨
§Insulin (controls rate of glucose)
  Inability to process glucose = Type 2 D.

Part III

What Can Help?

If you suffer from NES, you know how distressing it can be. Chapters 8 through 11 describe different types of night eating and the thoughts that are associated with each type. You are invited to become an active participant by linking the thoughts and behaviors associated with your night eating to the types we describe. In these chapters, several behavioral and relaxation strategies are explained and some medical treatments are explored.

Chapter 8

Help Yourself: Serving Up New Thought Patterns

Now that you know more about the different aspects of NES, we turn our attention to helping you to help yourself. Throughout the next two chapters we will focus on several different strategies, including behavioral tasks that you can try to carry out, cognitive approaches that aim at changing the negative thoughts that influence your emotions, and relaxation and stress-reduction techniques. First we will help you figure out what are the central thoughts and beliefs that may be influencing your NES.

In the diaries our patients keep, they record their thoughts before and after they eat at night so that they and we can gain more insight into their personal experiences with their late-night compulsions to eat. In the next couple of chapters, you will examine the thoughts you have before and after you eat, so that you can come to understand how your environment and your inner thoughts interact to maintain your night eating.

We must make one important point here. In earlier chapters we've described the physiological and genetic contributions to NES that are currently known. But even though these physical and genetic aspects may be influencing your behavior, this does not mean that you can't change your behavior. What it means is that it will take some extra work on your part to resist the established patterns that you have been living with and then to change them.

Four Types of Night Eating

From our patients' accounts, we have discovered that there are at least four different categories of NES:

1. the compelled evening and nighttime overeater

2. the anxious/agitated night eater

3. the cravings night eater

4. the all-or-nothing belief about sleep night eater

We will discuss these types more fully, and then describe helpful approaches for each one in the second half of this chapter.

The Compelled Evening and Nighttime Overeater

You have learned the three classic signs of NES are (1) not being hungry in the morning, (2) eating a very large part of your daily calories in the evening, and (3) getting up throughout the night to eat. In our work with NES patients, however, we discovered that about 15 percent of NES patients have the first two signs but they don't get up to eat in the middle of the night. Why are these patients still considered night eaters? The reason we consider this subgroup as having NES is due to their daily, or circadian, pattern of eating. That is, much of what they eat is consumed in the evening and nighttime. Many times patients from this subgroup stay up quite late, and after eating their evening meal they continue eating well into the night before they feel ready to fall asleep. They report feeling a compulsion to eat during the evening and nighttime hours. This compulsion can be so strong that they do not believe they will be able to fall asleep without eating the foods that they are craving. Each night eater has preferred foods. Some crave snack foods while others continue to eat leftovers from their evening meal.

If you are a compelled evening and nighttime eater, a characteristic rationalization you might use before eating in the evening or late night might go something like this: "That ice cream I had an hour ago was really good. I really want some more. I need some more. I *know* that if I don't eat it, there is no chance I'll fall asleep later on when I go to bed. Also, I hardly ate anything earlier today, so it's okay if I have more ice cream now." This chain of thought allows you to give yourself permission to go ahead and eat an extra bowl (or two!) of ice cream at a time when you really do not want to be eating.

After you've eaten the ice cream, you may have thoughts like these: "I can't believe I couldn't control myself again. I've been eating all night. I didn't really need another bowl. I am a bad person." Thoughts like these are often called *automatic thoughts.* They occur without much deliberation over their content, and you probably aren't even aware that you're having them. Yet, emotionally, they affect how you feel about yourself and your actions.

When we asked our patients to write down what they were thinking, many responded that they didn't think much at all about their nighttime eating; they just selected their food and ate it in an automatic fashion. Note that they didn't eat in an *unconscious* fashion. Unconscious eating would be categorized as nocturnal sleep-related eating disorder (NS-RED). However, when they were asked to stop and actually monitor their thoughts, they were able to remember many different statements they had been telling themselves, many of which were personally demeaning.

Several very different factors may influence your evening and nighttime overeating. We have already discussed the particular hormones that may be working within your body to influence your nighttime pattern of eating, but there are also environmental cues that help to maintain this pattern. What do you typically do during the evening? Do you watch TV? Do you spend time with your friends or family? Do you exercise? Do you get engaged in activities outside your home, such as a club or class?

If most of your evenings are spent at home with little to do but watch TV or engage in other solitary activities, your chances of eating at night increase. First, when you watch TV, you are bombarded by commercials for fast-food restaurants, enticing snacks, and many other appealing food advertisements. These ads stimulate your appetite at a time when you, as a night eater, are already cued to eat. Second, if you are bored and not very absorbed mentally in an activity, then you are also more likely to eat. Finally, if you live alone, you may lack social support and group activities that could help you cut down on your nighttime eating. With no one else around, you may feel less inhibited about your food choices and portion sizes. Each of these issues may play into your own struggle with NES, and you are sure to have additional, unique situations that cue your eating.

Exercise: Describe Your Personal Cues to Eat at Night

If you identify with the compelled evening and nighttime overeater type, take out your journal now and try to describe some of your personal cues or vulnerable situations for eating in the evening or at night.

The Anxious/Agitated Night Eater

When you wake at night, you probably don't pay much attention to your thoughts, because most likely you're groggy, even a bit confused. You may think that your body is on autopilot each night as you make your trip from your bed to the kitchen. However, even in this sleepy state, you are still having the type of automatic thoughts discussed above.

Anxiety-associated contemplation may be one type of thinking you engage in during your eating expeditions. You may refer back to a situation that you experienced earlier in the day, or think about an ongoing stressful situation. For example, a typical thought might be, "I can't clear my mind. I'm having flashbacks of too many memories from my fight with my husband today. Eating will calm me down, and I will be able to sleep again."

Many times, if you awaken with anxious thoughts running through your mind, you also may feel physically agitated and stressed. You may be unable to lie still in bed and may feel as though you'll never fall back to sleep on your own. Ultimately, you end up turning to food. You know from past experience that eating some food comforts and soothes you. You can focus on the food—the taste, the texture, and the feeling of fullness—and not on the problems hanging over you.

Your physical agitation, which takes the form of feeling restless, having an increased heart rate, and breathing quickly and shallowly, is a by-product of your anxiety and it may show itself in other ways, too. When you are up at night looking for your favorite foods, do you feel angry or say things to loved ones that you would not usually say? Does anyone or anything that comes between you and your food suffer the consequences? If your spouse, child, or roommate tries to stop you from eating, do you make a nasty comment or become belligerent? If you've posted signs on the refrigerator or erected physical barriers to stop your eating, you may angrily rip the signs down and carelessly shove the barriers out of your path. In this state, you don't want to listen to reason, either your own or that of your housemates. Instead, you just want the food that will soothe you and that you have learned will help to put you back to sleep.

Exercise: Describe the Anxiety-Provoking Thoughts That Cause You to Eat at Night

Do you have anxiety-provoking thoughts during the night? Do they drive you to eat? If you do, take out your journal now, and start writing down what these thoughts are, and describe how much they influence your nighttime eating behaviors. Try to write out your thoughts in as much detail as you can.

The Cravings Night Eater

The cravings type of night eater experiences cravings similar to those that some people have for drugs or alcohol. However, the cravings we are discussing are not physical, but psychological. The act of eating your favorite foods makes you feel good and relaxed, which reinforces your reasons for night eating in the future. In this type of NES, the main purpose of the night eating is mostly to satisfy your cravings, the strong drive you have to eat certain foods; helping yourself fall back to sleep is only a secondary motive.

We're sure you know some people who complain that they are addicted to certain foods, and not just those who have NES. For example, carbohydrates are a common type of food that people say they are addicted to. The Food and Drug Administration (FDA) recommends that about 50 percent of our calories should come from carbohydrates. Many forms of carbohydrates are good for us, such as fruits and vegetables. However, many snack foods are as flavorful as they are because they are made of refined sugars and bleached flour. The appealing flavor triggers a part of your brain that registers these snacks as rewards, and you want to eat more and more of them.

The thoughts of one patient with this craving type of NES included these: "I'm tired, but I want something sweet, so I'll go and get it now. I shouldn't be eating it, but it will taste so good, and I really need to experience that taste to feel better. Oh well,

I'll try not to do it again." After she ate her snack, she wrote, "Now I feel bad and I think, 'I shouldn't have eaten that.' Then I get real blue and say to myself, 'You need to really do something to stop this, because you are too fat.'" You can see from this example that her experience of eating sweets as rewards in the past encourages her to eat those foods again.

She does not consider the consequences before she eats, but her diary entry makes her distress clear. Afterward, not only did the snack not provide any lasting feeling of comfort, but she actually felt physically ill. (Late-night eating makes you feel this way, especially if it gives you acid reflux and indigestion.) Then she became conscious of the fact that the extra calories she had just consumed were working against her goal of losing weight.

Exercise: After Eating at Night, Describe How It Made You Feel

Start keeping your journal available so that you can review how distressing the experience of eating at night is—both physically and emotionally. Plan to keep your journal beside your bed or in your kitchen. Once you've finished a bout of night eating, it is a good time to start reflecting on the ill effects of your eating.

If you can't write in your journal immediately after a night eating episode because you are too sleepy, then write about the event first thing in the morning. Writing down these thoughts and rereading what you've written will help you to form clearer memories of these episodes. Eventually, these memories will start to act as a deterrent to your late snacking.

The All-or-Nothing Belief about Sleep Night Eater

The person who has the fourth type of NES focuses primarily on thoughts and beliefs about the effects of not getting enough sleep. We've all had the rule drilled into our heads that we should get eight hours of sleep each night. In general, this is a good rule to live by, but what happens when you can only manage to get six hours of sleep, or even as little as four or five hours?

Although some people do fine on five hours of sleep, most of us do not; and lack of sleep can adversely affect our physical and mental health over the long term. Since you are well aware that night eaters have interrupted sleep patterns, you may be curious about how much of a sleep deficit, if any, night eaters experience. We also wanted to know that, so we measured the number of hours of sleep that people with night eating get compared to the amount of sleep that people without NES get.

We used three different methods to make sure our measurements were correct, including self-reports in patient sleep diaries, motion sensor watches, and polysomnography (see chapter 3). To our surprise, on average, people in both groups studied actually slept the same total number of hours! Remember, this is on average, and your experience differs both from another person's experience, and varies from night to night. In general, the time it takes people with NES to wake up and eat and then fall back to sleep is about twenty minutes. Although you would expect these awakenings to reduce the number of the total hours slept, people with NES usually make up this time by sleeping a little bit later than those without the syndrome.

Even if you are getting enough sleep overall, when you wake up in the middle of the night and find it difficult just to roll over and go back to sleep, you end up feeling awful. These feelings are both physical and mental. People with this type of NES may think when they wake up, "I'm so tired and I can't sleep. If I just eat something, I'll be able to sleep. My stomach is bugging me. If I don't eat something to quiet it, I will just keep on getting up, and I'll never get enough sleep to function tomorrow."

You can see how this all-or-nothing belief differs from the craving type, in which the food is the primary focus and sleep is secondary. In the all-or-nothing thought pattern, the focus on getting enough sleep is in the forefront of the person's thoughts. Food is just the means to the end; these night eaters believe that eating will relax them and they will be able to resume their precious sleep. After they finish eating, they focus on sleep again, "Hope I can sleep through until morning. I'm very tired. I just need to sleep all the way through. I don't want to have to get up again."

This person's thoughts are similar to those that someone with classic insomnia would have. Most people with classic insomnia do not eat when they wake up at night, but they start having anxious thoughts about not getting enough sleep. Then they start thinking about how the lack of sleep will affect their performance at work, their interest in social activities, and their relationships. The more they think these thoughts, the higher their anxiety rises, and the less likely they are to fall back to sleep.

People with NES who have these kinds of thoughts about sleep have found that, as a rule, eating something will soothe and relax them, so they can fall back asleep. In this way, eating becomes a conditioned response to waking, and they are "hooked" on night eating. In fact, with night eaters, eating seems to work better than taking a sleeping pill. Our patients have told us this again and again.

How Your Thoughts Affect Your Nighttime Eating

While it may not seem apparent to you, your thoughts play a big role in most of what you do. Your body performs many functions automatically, such as digesting food, pumping blood, breathing, processing visual cues, hearing, and sneezing. However, a large part of your behavior is governed by decisions, such as whether or not to stop the car at a stoplight, what to wear each day, and whether or not to make that sarcastic comment about someone's behavior.

Eating during the night may seem as automatic to you as breathing, as it has probably become part of your nightly routine. However, there are steps along the way, and decisions you make about these steps, whether you are aware of them or not. When you perform a task over and over again, the decision-making process doesn't seem so apparent. For example, when you first learn to ride a bike, you are very aware of all of the different things you have to do: look where you are going, make sure your body is balanced, and that you pedal at the right speed. After you have these basics down, you no longer consciously think about each step in the process. You just ride your bike. If your night eating has become routine, you probably don't think about the steps associated with it either. So, now, we will take a look at these automatic thoughts and behaviors and try to raise your awareness about each step you take when you get up from sleeping to eat at night.

Your Nighttime Eating Chain

Picture your nighttime eating routine as a chain. There is a series of events that occur each time you eat. Although your routine may vary slightly, you probably follow a pretty similar routine each night. You can think of it like this:

1 • The first link occurs when you wake.

2 • The second link consists of the automatic thoughts that begin to crowd your head.

3 • The third and fourth links take place when you get up from your bed and make your way to your kitchen.

4 • Links five and six occur when you choose what to eat, and then you eat what you chose.

5 • On link seven you make your way back to your bed.

6 • Link eight finds you going back to sleep.

You may have a few extra links in your chain, like stopping to use the bathroom or taking your dog out for a walk. You might also watch a little TV or read while you eat. In any case, the essential steps, or links, are laid out above.

You may not even be aware that you are making a decision at each link of the chain. Our goal is to help you become aware of these links and then to start breaking them. At first, this can be very difficult, but the more aware you become of each of the separate steps you take, the easier it will be to find the weakest link, change it, or break it completely.

For instance, take link five from above—choosing what to eat. You might think that you don't make a conscious decision about what to eat while you are up. You may believe that you automatically pick anything. In fact, you probably are not completely aware of the decision process that you go through at that time of night. However, consider this: If your food choices during your night eating episodes are so automatic, why don't you reach for broccoli and spinach as often as you reach for cookies or peanut butter?

Of course, if you have nocturnal sleep-related eating disorder (NS-RED), which was discussed in chapter 5, then you actually are sleepwalking while you are eating, and you will eat all kinds of foods and nonfoods. However, with NES, you are awake and have at least a groggy awareness of your actions.

Usually, it doesn't seem that you have the ability to control your food choices. However, you do, and the first step toward change is raising your level of awareness about each of the links in your chain. The patients in our studies were certainly amazed to learn that they were having these thoughts drive their eating.

You may be just as amazed to learn that you are having similar thoughts.

Exercise: What Are the Links in Your Chain?

- Now, in your journal, start a fresh page and write down each link on your nightly chain. List each step separately.

Raising Awareness about Automatic Thoughts in the Evening

Now that you have written down the series of behaviors that you perform each night in your night eating routine, let's examine the thoughts that accompany your behaviors. It is very important to write down your thoughts, so keeping your journal close at hand is essential. You should already be keeping track of your food intake, so now we are going to add a space next to or below where you write your food in your journal. This space will capture your thoughts.

Exercise: Capturing Your Thoughts

- Turn your journal horizontally.

- Along top of the page, write the following six column heads:

(1) Time

(2) Thoughts before Eating

(3) Food/Beverage Consumed

(4) Amount/Quantity

(5) Calories

(6) Thoughts after Eating

Columns 2 and 6 should be given the widest amount of space on the page because you will be doing the most writing in them. You may also choose to keep a blank page next to your food diary to expand on these thoughts.

- To begin changing your nighttime eating, set an *off-limits time* for eating. Pick a time after which you do not want to eat. After this time, try not to go into the kitchen or wherever else you keep your food. For some, this time may be as early as 8:00 P.M.; for others, it will be later. This will depend on when you and your family eat your evening meal and on other activities that may go on in your household, such as making lunches for the next day or cleaning up the kitchen.

- Every time that you eat after your off-limits time, record your thoughts in your journal—both before and after you eat. Yes, we know this can be a lot of work. But in a sense, that is the exactly the point. The more work you have to do to eat, the less appealing and rewarding eating will become for you.

- If you find that you are not physically hungry when you are reaching for your nighttime snack, try to think about the reasons why you want to eat. Are you bored? Is your favorite food too readily available in the kitchen? Was there a trigger, such as just seeing an appetizing commercial on TV?

- After you assess your reasons for eating, think of something else you might do for fifteen minutes to distract yourself from eating, perhaps you can read a magazine, talk to someone on the phone, or do the dishes.

- Reassess how strong your cravings are after those fifteen minutes have passed.

- If your cravings still seem unbearable, try to refocus your attention onto another task, or have a drink of water or a low-calorie drink. If this still isn't satisfying, have a small serving of a snack. However, taking only a small portion and resisting the urge to eat more is very difficult for most people.

- You may want to enlist someone else to help you stop at your pre-set quantity if you do choose to have a taste of your snack.

Raising Awareness about Automatic Thoughts When You Wake at Night

Recognizing your automatic thoughts during the late evening and nighttime hours before you go to sleep will be difficult, but catching those thoughts and writing them down in your journal when you wake to eat at night may be even more challenging. How difficult it will be depends on how aware or conscious you are when you awaken.

When do you first realize that you are awake? We have learned from our patients that there is a wide range of responses to this question. Some people say that they are wide awake while still in bed and they immediately become preoccupied with worries from the preceding day. If you are awake and aware from this early point, then you should be able to record many of the thoughts you are having.

On the other hand, some people say they are not aware that they have gotten out of bed until they are standing in front of the refrigerator or kitchen pantry. If this is the case, then your chances to record your thoughts will be more limited, but not impossible. Remember, the more you train yourself to research your own behaviors, the more aware of your behaviors you will become. If you have trouble writing neatly at night and want to keep scrap paper in the kitchen (or wherever you eat at night), that can work, too. But be sure and transfer whatever you write on the scrap paper into your journal the next day so your thoughts are written in an organized way. This way you will be able to review all of your notes easily.

The more you train yourself to really take notice of your behaviors and the thoughts associated with them, the earlier in your chain of behaviors you will become aware of them. Give yourself some time to get used to this process. If at first you are able to capture only the thoughts you have after you eat, then start there. You will still gain great insights from doing just this step. When you are able, focus your attention on the thoughts that come before your night eating. As time goes by, seeing your thoughts written down on paper will help you to see the big picture, instead of seeing your night eating as just an isolated behavior unrelated to the other stressors and issues in your life.

Examining and Evaluating Your Thoughts

When you have some pages of notes of your thoughts, it's time to examine their logic. Let's examine a thought like, "I need to get up and eat something right now. I can't stand this craving any longer." How true is it that you need to eat something at that moment? What would happen if you didn't eat? Would your hunger pangs become intolerable? Would you be unable to fall back to sleep? The only way to learn the true answers to these questions is to test them out. Have you lain in bed before without acting on the urge to eat at night? If so, how long were you able to fight your craving? Five minutes? Two hours? All night?

We are asking you to experiment with your usual chain of behaviors. For instance, if you normally wake up and immediately get out of bed, make yourself wait at least five minutes. At the end of those five minutes, reassess your craving. If it has lessened, see if you can wait another five minutes. Keep reassessing your cravings. Only then will you know if they are so intolerable that you absolutely must get up to eat something.

If your cravings overwhelm you, plan to change another part of your chain by trying to limit the quantity of what you eat. It will help to have something premeasured waiting for you that you prepared before you went to bed. You will know that everything else is off-limits. This may be difficult, but as you continue to keep records of your thoughts, you will see how overindulging affects you, perhaps by increasing your feelings of guilt, depression, or anxiety.

You will also see that successfully eating smaller amounts at night can increase your feelings of self-efficacy and accomplishment. The more you expose yourself to the negative consequences of your night eating episodes, the more rewarding eating a smaller portion will become.

As limiting your snacking becomes easier, we suggest that you try having some water or a low-calorie drink instead of food. This may take some time, but in the long run, you will wean yourself from unhealthy eating and replace it with low-calorie substitutes. Not only will substituting something healthier than your favorite, high-calorie nighttime food help you to feel better about yourself, it also won't add as many pounds. Moreover, if you have problems with indigestion, acid reflux, or any other digestive problems, these discomforts are likely to diminish as you decrease your night eating.

How Your Thoughts Influence Your Emotions

As discussed in earlier chapters, many people with NES experience feelings of depression. Feeling depressed is just one of many emotions you may have as a result of your night eating. Other feelings may include guilt, anxiety, and sadness. Initially, after eating, you may feel calmed and content, but, as a rule, these feelings usually change into the more negative emotions and thoughts just listed, especially if you are already distressed by your pattern of nighttime eating.

Some people who develop NES may feel bad immediately after their nightly trips to the kitchen, while it can take years of such trips to bother others. If you are reading this book, however, you are most likely experiencing enough distress for you to consider making changes.

Earlier in this chapter you learned more about the automatic thoughts you experience during your night eating. These thoughts directly influence your feelings. So, even if you have trouble identifying and articulating your thoughts during the night, you probably will have thoughts about your behaviors the following day. These thoughts are very important to note and examine, because the emotions you experience as a result of your automatic thoughts during the day may be interfering with your daily functioning to an even greater extent than those you experience at night.

For many people, identifying their emotions is an easier task than identifying the particular thoughts that go with them. For example, you may realize that you are feeling mad at yourself, which, in turn, leads you to take that anger out on others around you. However, you might not stop to think about the reason you are mad at yourself. If you did, you might discover that you were having thoughts like, "I look terrible. I keep gaining weight because I have no control over my night eating. I should be able to stop myself from pigging out in the middle of the night. I'm such a loser!"

Chain Reactions

The principle that emotions and thoughts are intimately linked is a key idea in the field of psychotherapy. An event will lead first to an emotion, and the emotion to a thought, and the thought to a behavior. Your automatic thoughts usually are based on your interpretation of an event.

For example, Joe has been trying to diet. One of the rules he is trying to follow is not to eat any cakes or cookies. However, there is carrot cake, his favorite kind, at the office for a colleague's birthday celebration. He eats a piece. He feels guilty and interprets this as failing. In turn, he generalizes this one small failure to his whole dieting effort, even though he had been doing very well all that week. Subsequently, he continues to eat sweets the rest of the day, which derails his efforts even more.

You can see the connection here between the event (eating cake), Joe's emotion (guilt), his thoughts (I'm a failure), and the resulting behavior (eating even more unplanned calories). Think about how this scenario might have yielded different results if Joe had taken a minute to examine his automatic thoughts and tried to change them.

Joe's interpretation of eating the cake was a highly personal one; that he was a failure, specifically at dieting, but perhaps on a deeper level as well. Now think of how a friend or his spouse might have thought about his situation. Perhaps they would have thought that he could cut down on his food intake for the rest of his meals for that day or the next. The thought that he was a failure probably wouldn't even cross their minds.

Thus, when you are thinking about how to change your automatic thoughts, it often is helpful to put yourself in someone else's shoes, as an observer of your situation—either real or imagined. An observer's automatic thoughts are usually less judgmental and may be less detrimental to your mood and your overall functioning.

So catching your automatic thoughts, as discussed earlier in this chapter's journal exercises, is the first step. Whether you need to identify your emotion first, and then identify the automatic thoughts associated with the emotion, is up to you, depending on how easily you can identify your automatic thoughts. As we said, sometimes your emotions are more obvious to you and are an easier place to start. Either way, the main goal is to start to change the thoughts you have so that your behaviors can change. As you can see, automatic thoughts and emotions feed into each other and are part of an endless cycle that affects your behaviors.

Imagine how the outcome of Joe's situation would have been different if he had been able to catch his automatic thought of "I'm a loser," and insert a new thought in its place. Suppose he had thought, "I'm not happy that I ate that cake, but I will just cut down on my other meals today to make up for it." If he had been able to take this step, he might not have fallen off the dieting wagon in the first place (the resulting behavior), and he would have felt better emotionally in the end, as well.

Exercise: Change Your NES by Changing Your Thoughts and Emotions

- Take a look at the thoughts you've recorded in your journal when you've eaten after your off-limits time and when you've awakened to eat at night.

- Take a moment to recall your emotions at those times, if you haven't noted those already.

- Then, take a moment to experience your current emotions as you review your journal.

- As you let yourself experience these emotions, be mindful of any automatic thoughts that pop up. Now is an excellent time to start changing those thoughts.

For example, if while reviewing your journal entries you thought, "This will be impossible to change. I've been getting up to eat for so long. I just don't know how I will overcome it," then you are probably feeling discouraged, depressed, or anxious. How can you change that thought to give yourself the motivation you need to change and to make yourself feel better?

One alternative response could be, "Okay. I have my work cut out for me. This will be challenging, but if I really try to examine the chain of steps that I take each night to eat, and the thoughts I have that control those steps, then I can start to break the chain." Reframing your internal dialogue can give you the motivation you need to change your eating patterns; it also can change your emotional state of mind. The end result will find you with a more positive attitude about yourself and your ability to change, which, in turn, will give you a more positive outlook on your ability to interact with others, perform well at your job, and generally improve your sense of self-efficacy. It will increase your ability to achieve what you want to achieve.

This Chapter's Goals

- Keep your journal close at hand. Start a new page to describe your nighttime eating "chain of behaviors" by identifying each separate step you take.

- Write down your thoughts before and after you eat during your off-limits time and during the night. Try to identify which type of night eating thoughts you have most frequently.

- Examine how those automatic thoughts influence your emotions, and how, in turn, they influence how much and how often you eat.

- Review your journal during the day to generate alternative responses to your automatic thoughts so that this process becomes easier for you to do during the night.

CHAPTER 9

Imagery, Relaxation, and Behavioral Interventions

Knowing what type of thoughts and beliefs you have regarding your night eating will help you understand how to improve your own situation. If you haven't read chapter 8 recently, you may want to give it a quick review so that you are familiar with the four different types of mindsets associated with night eating. They are: the evening and nighttime overeater, the anxious/agitated night eater, the cravings night eater, and the all-or-nothing belief about sleep night eater. In this chapter, we will discuss different approaches to battling your night eating and point out those that may be most helpful for each subtype of NES.

Structured Mealtimes and Snacks

As discussed in chapter 2, many people with NES don't have regular meal and snack times. For example, you probably don't eat breakfast, or you have only a bite of something. Then you may eat a late lunch. By midafternoon, your snacking probably increases. You may eat a large evening meal, and for those of you with evening and nighttime overeating, you find yourself "grazing" until you go to bed.

We've heard from some NES sufferers that they are the picture of restraint and controlled eating during the day. But, when it comes to NES, this so-called restraint may not be as positive a behavior as it seems. If controlled eating is how you would describe your daytime routine, there are still aspects of your eating pattern that can and probably should be adjusted. As you cut down on your night eating episodes, you should increase your breakfast intake. Eating a balanced breakfast may help to curb your appetite for uncontrolled snacking throughout the day.

Do you restrict your food intake throughout the day, knowing that later on you'll have your evening, nighttime, or nocturnal eating episodes? During the day, without the energy that food provides to sustain you, you may turn to drinking caffeinated drinks to keep you going. How much caffeine do you consume each day? Do you drink several cups of coffee, tea, or caffeinated cold beverages, such as colas or iced tea? If so, your caffeine intake could keep you awake at night, making it harder to fall asleep or stay asleep. We'll go into greater detail about this later in the chapter.

As discussed in chapter 2, structuring your mealtimes and snack times is a good start for overcoming night eating. Set up regular times to eat breakfast, lunch, an afternoon snack, and your evening meal. As your night eating decreases and you regain your appetite throughout the day, you also may want to plan a time for a midmorning snack. After your evening meal, plan to eat a single snack before you go to bed.

Exercise: Restructure Your Eating Schedule

- Begin with modest goals. Start by allowing yourself the snacks you usually eat that you know will satisfy you.

- Remember to write down your thoughts in your journal before and after you eat during this time, particularly if you eat a snack during your off-limits time (as discussed in chapter 8).

- After a week of maintaining a set time and amount for your evening snack food, begin to decrease the portion size.

- If your usual snack food is high in calories, try a new, lower-calorie substitute. For example, if you are eating cookies and whole milk, switch to low-calorie cookies and low-fat or skim milk.

- Your eventual goal should be to decrease your evening eating to a single, healthy snack.

If you are not used to eating low-fat or low-calorie foods, we know that you may be thinking, "How can those foods possibly be satisfying?" Many people who haven't tried these foods resist the idea of eating reduced-calorie foods. Their most common complaint is the taste. If you try some, you may find that you actually like the taste of some diet foods or drinks better than the high-calorie ones, but with others, getting used to the taste could take a few weeks, possibly a month or more. This is where you have to make a decision. What is more important to you, getting used to the taste of these new foods and drinks, or continuing on with your old favorites?

Some of the new foods you'll choose may have sugar substitutes as an ingredient. One common concern and misconception about sugar substitutes is that these products may cause cancer. Early studies on laboratory animals suggested this might be the case. However, these animals were given up to 500 times more saccharine than a human could possibly consume (Schiffman and Gatlin 1993). More recent studies show no link between sugar substitutes and cancer. In fact, the link between being overweight or obese and suffering or dying from cancer are more clear-cut than any link ever reported between cancer and artificial sweeteners, even among laboratory animals (Calle et al. 2003).

Remember, start with modest goals when you restructure your eating schedule. If right now you're saying to yourself, "But I don't have time to eat breakfast or lunch during the day," then take a second look at your schedule. In chapter 4 you learned that NES is not only an eating disorder, it is also a stress-related disorder. So if you are working too hard to eat breakfast and take a thirty-minute, or even a twenty-minute break to eat lunch, your overall health and well-being will continue to be negatively affected.

We recognize that restructuring your meal times will not be easy. Nothing about changing your night eating patterns will be easy. When a planned change doesn't work out, you may feel worse about yourself and more likely to give up on any further efforts to change. That's why it's important to start with small, realistic goals. Lifestyle changes need to be carried out in small, incremental steps for the behaviors to become integrated into your daily routines and your life for the long haul.

Stimulus Control

So, what are the steps to help you go about limiting yourself to less frequent and healthier snacks? One simple step is to use stimulus control, or, in plain English, don't keep the forbidden foods in your home. *Stimulus control* means limiting your exposure to the foods you like to eat. This strategy is helpful for all types of night eaters, but probably most specifically for the evening and nighttime overeaters and the cravings night eaters. However, as discussed in chapter 8, food is not the only thing that acts as a trigger signaling you to eat. Other stimuli, or situations, could provoke you to begin to graze.

Where do you eat your evening and nighttime snacks? Do you eat them in the kitchen, or do you have a favorite chair in your family room where you sit and snack? Do you have food readily available in that place? The goal of stimulus control is to have one designated place where you eat your meals and snacks. Usually, this would be at your dinner table or in your kitchen.

≠
bed

Exercise: Your Designated Eating Place

- A designated eating place might be your dining table or the table in your kitchen. Wherever that place may be, designate it as *your* eating place and try never to eat anywhere else in your home.

- If you are sitting in your favorite chair in front of the television and you would like a snack, remember to eat it in your designated eating area. If you are truly hungry, then getting up from your chair won't seem like too much effort.

- If you want to eat because you are bored or for some other reason, then getting up to go to your designated eating place will seem to take more effort.

- The extra effort will also give you a chance to evaluate just how hungry you really are.

Although an important step in controlling your stimuli successfully is not to consume food at your former grazing spots, there is one exception to this rule. First, we are assuming that you haven't selected your bed as your designated area, and, if you have, we strongly encourage you to rethink your choice. As you decrease the amount you eat when you wake at night, we do encourage you to keep a small snack by your bedside to (1) limit your choices for your nighttime snack and (2) keep you from getting up and out of bed to snack. This doesn't mean that we want you to keep an unlimited number of snacks in your room. In fact, we want you to keep only your small, chosen snack there when you go to bed. Don't choose a snack that smells particularly attractive or it will be so irresistible you will eat it before you go to sleep. We discuss the progression of limiting your nocturnal snacking later in this chapter.

Restraint and Exposure

For many people, there are foods that you think of as "forbidden foods." Usually, these foods are commercially prepared snacks or sweets, such as cookies, cakes, or candy. These foods taste so good and, thus, are so rewarding, that many people have a difficult time stopping with a preplanned quantity of them. Therefore, they try to stay away from, or *restrict*, such foods completely. However, these foods are often present in your home or the office snack machines, or they're offered to you by a friend.

If you *plan* to avoid these foods totally, and then you *decide* to go ahead and have some in spite of your plan, you may find that it is even more difficult to stop yourself from eating a larger portion than you had planned. This, in turn, can lead you to feel badly about your efforts at self-control, and even worse about yourself as a person.

The consequence of these negative feelings may well be another episode of overeating, or possibly a day, week, or month of overeating. If you see this kind of eating as a lack of willpower, it may provoke you to give up trying to change your eating patterns altogether. Don't allow lapses in control like this to derail all your efforts.

To help guard yourself from indulging in your forbidden foods, you will use a technique called *exposure*. The idea is that you allow yourself to experience the forbidden food in a gradual, or graded, fashion. First, you introduce the food at a safe time, and then you increase the amount of temptation you feel by placing yourself in increasingly difficult situations. Your goal is to be able to eat a reasonable amount of the troublesome food at more vulnerable times. With each step you take, you also monitor the thoughts that you have about that food and create a rational dialogue with yourself about the pros and cons of eating it. To try this technique, follow the exercise below.

Exercise: Taking Control over Your Forbidden Foods

The following exercise is the first step to introduce yourself to a *graded exposure* to your forbidden foods.

1. To control your eating of tempting foods, introduce them into your diet when you are not very hungry.

2. Allow yourself a small portion of the desired food after you have eaten a regular meal. If you are already satiated, you will be less likely to overeat these empty calories, yet you will still be getting a taste of the food.

3. With your desire for a taste satisfied, you will have less reason to eat these foods when you are more vulnerable, for example, when you are very hungry or when your self-control is impaired upon awakening to eat. If you go ahead and eat these foods on an empty stomach, you are setting yourself up for an overeating episode. Such episodes will have negative effects on your mood, weight, and self-esteem.

4. Once you feel comfortable eating these foods in small portions on a full stomach, you can introduce these foods into different situations. For example, when you feel comfortable eating a small portion after a meal, you will learn to be able to feel satisfied with a similar portion when offered a piece of cake at birthday party, or when a friend offers you some candy while you are at the movies together.

This strategy should help your eating during the day and before you go to bed. However, a different, more stringent form of exposure may be useful to handle your nocturnal snacking.

Exposure for Nocturnal Eating Episodes

Many of our patients report that they are vulnerable to eating specific foods, such as peanut butter, ice cream, chips, or cookies during the night. In contrast, they say they don't have as much difficulty resisting these foods during the day. Therefore, it will be easiest for you to work first on techniques to resist these foods when you have the most control, that is, during the daytime. Then, once you have gained some confidence in your new skills, you can try to apply them to help yourself resist those foods that you eat at night when your self-control is at its lowest.

Imagery

The exposure technique is often combined with the use of imagery. The goal of using imagery and exposure together is to make the situation you imagine as real as you can while you gradually learn to overcome your cravings for the desired foods.

The first step of this process is to imagine the foods that you crave at a time when you feel physically full and in control. For example, imagine a jar of your favorite peanut butter or any of your favorite foods. Imagine everything about it: how it looks, smells, tastes, and feels as you eat it. Are you beginning to want some of it? You just created a food craving with this experience of imagery.

How can you go about resisting this craving? Well, hopefully, you didn't just put the book down and go to the kitchen to get a jar of peanut butter. If you are still reading, then you've resisted that initial craving. Good for you!

How Hungry Are You?

Let's take another look at how hungry you are right now. If you started this exercise with a full stomach, then you should still be full, despite your craving for the favorite food. At this time, that craving is more of a psychological process than a physical one. So why do you still want the food? Because you know it will taste good.

Before you give in to the urge to satisfy your craving and have a taste of your favorite food, stop to think for a minute about how you will feel—physically and psychologically—after eating it. We know that you will feel good while eating the food; it will taste good and take away the thoughts that we and you created with this exercise. But now imagine how you will feel fifteen minutes after you've eaten the food.

Since you are already physically full, it may make you feel physically uncomfortable. You may be able to remember this feeling from another overeating episode. Draw on that experience. When this sensation hits, your thoughts and feelings will turn negative. You may become angry with yourself, or you may become depressed. You may think, "I've just eaten a lot of extra calories. They will make me gain more weight." Or, you could take it further and think, "I've failed again! I can't control my eating, even though I wasn't really hungry." These thoughts, in turn, may lead you to think of other aspects of your life in which you didn't succeed.

So, you can see it's a good idea to do the exercise described below when you aren't hungry and are in a controlled setting. It's also important to follow each of the steps listed below in order. Considering the thoughts and feelings you'll have when you finish the exercise is very important, since this will provide the motivation (as unpleasant as it may be) for you to resist the psychological craving for food.

Exercise: Imagery Steps

1. Imagine your favorite nighttime foods. Imagine their taste and smell and the way it feels to eat these foods.

2. Think about how you will feel immediately after you eat these foods.

3. Think carefully about how much physical hunger you have. Even if you are craving a food psychologically, if you are not physically hungry, remind yourself that this is a good reason not to eat anything.

4. Think about how you will feel fifteen minutes after eating these foods. Let yourself experience the negative reaction you will inevitably have. The more fully you let yourself experience the negative consequences, the more you will be able to resist your cravings.

The Next Step

Move on to this next step only when you feel comfortable resisting the cravings you create from your imagery exercises. The next step is to place your favorite food in front of you. You will go through the same steps as in the exercise above, except that now, instead of imagining your favorite food, actually place it in front of you. The goal is to practice until you can resist eating the food in front of you.

Exercise: Resisting Your Favorite Food When It Is in Front of You

1. The key to being able to resist is that thinking about the negative experience and the distress you'll feel after eating these extra calories should outweigh the temporary positive experience you would have if you ate the food.

2. You also will begin to understand that just because you have a psychological craving for the food, doesn't mean that you automatically have to eat it.

3. What do you think will happen to you if you don't eat the snack? The truth is, you will survive without those extra bites.

4. Once you have convinced yourself not to eat the food, move on to another activity, such as reading or taking a walk (or, in this case, continue reading this book). Distract yourself and change your thoughts to another topic beyond eating or food.

Resisting at Night and the Next Step

Once you feel comfortable and have achieved some success with this exercise during the day, try doing it at off-limits times and at night. During these times, you won't have to create the craving artificially. It will occur naturally.

When the craving hits you at night, go through the same steps you practiced during the day. You will be more vulnerable at this time, so try hard to fully imagine the negative consequences of your eating before you *decide* whether or not to eat. We stress the word "decide" here, because, no matter how strong the cravings are, you really do have a choice about whether to eat or not.

When you practiced the steps during the day, it was during times that you weren't physically hungry. This will likely be different at night. If you experience physical feelings of hunger, they may be stronger than your psychological craving.

Exercise: Resisting Cravings at Night

1. If you do experience feelings of hunger, you can still walk through the steps of the imagery exercise.

2. Then, if the craving is still overwhelming, allow yourself to have an appropriately sized serving of the snack.

3. While you are allowing yourself to eat this small snack, continue to use imagery to work on your self-control. Think especially about how badly you will feel if you eat more of the snack than you feel is appropriate.

4. This is where your psychological cravings may come to the forefront and override the physical sensation of hunger.

5. Remember, as you read in chapter 2, you should stop eating for at least ten minutes before you decide to eat another bite of your desired food.

6. After ten to twenty minutes, you will be able to sense better if you are still physically hungry. If you are not hungry anymore, stop eating.

7. If you are still physically hungry, have another small serving, and wait ten to twenty minutes again to see whether you are physically satisfied.

We know that these exercises are more difficult in practice than in theory, so hang in there. Remember, set modest goals, and don't give up if you are not successful right away. You won't be able to master this technique immediately. Undoubtedly you will have setbacks along the way, lapses in your ability to control yourself. Don't let those setbacks become a reason to quit. You *can* change your night eating habits. It will be a lot of work, but keep in mind how much better you will feel when you are eating less and less at night.

As your body adjusts to these new patterns, the effort you consciously have to put into it will lessen. Again, it's just like learning to ride a bike; eventually you will be able to do it with much less effort. Think about what it feels like when you are riding a bike in a lot of traffic. Maneuvering the bike, the whole complex process of balancing, pedaling, and steering may become more difficult and may require you to pay attention to the basic mechanics of bike riding again.

Similarly, when life is more stressful, your urge to eat at night may resurface stronger than ever, and you may have to return to the basics and walk through these exercises again. These emotional challenges serve to remind you of just how important it is for you to resist eating at night, because of how lousy it will make you feel in the end.

Relaxation

The stress-related component of NES may cause you to feel anxious or tense in the evening when you are trying to fall asleep or when you wake in the middle of the night. The tension and anxiety can make your night eating worse in two ways: (1) it can cause you to seek food as a way to comfort yourself, and (2) it can interfere with your ability to fall asleep or stay asleep. Thus, anxiety can be linked to food cravings as well as to insomnia.

People have many different ways to unwind after a stressful day. However, most people don't have the time (or won't make the time) to do what works best for them. This may include taking a hot bath, talking on the phone with a friend who makes you laugh, or spending some romantic time with your partner or spouse. Relaxation exercises are particularly effective for a few reasons. First, your ability to use them is not dependent on anyone else's schedule or help. You can do them by yourself. Second, you don't need elaborate equipment or lots of space to do them. Third, generally, you won't be disturbing other people in your household when you do relaxation exercises, even at night. As you can see, there's really no reason why they can't be done with some regularity.

There are several different types of relaxation exercises. We will review two of the most popular: breathing and progressive muscle relaxation. Both have been used widely to treat eating and sleeping problems. In fact, research has shown that even a week's worth of daily progressive muscle relaxation can reduce not only stress, anxiety, fatigue, anger, and depression, but it also decreases night eating episodes and begins to increase morning hunger (Pawlow, O'Neil, and Malcolm 2003).

Breathing

Breathing is the first necessity for life. It is, however, such an automatic function that we don't give it much attention as we go about our daily activities. But how you breathe can influence many aspects of your functioning. You may know that how you breathe affects your ability to carry out physical tasks, such as climbing stairs, jogging, or lifting the groceries. What you may not realize is that the way you breathe also can affect your emotions.

When you are on edge, either because of a scare or an anxiety-provoking situation, your body responds. You've probably noticed that when you are afraid or anxious, you start to breathe faster. You might not have noticed that your breathing also becomes shallower. When you breathe in a shallow way, your chest muscles are doing the work, not your abdominal muscles, which cause deep breathing. When your breathing is shallow, your shoulders move up as you inhale, a sure sign that you're breathing from your chest muscles.

Shallow Breathing and Panic Attacks

Shallow breathing is associated with increased heart rate and muscle tension. Some people experience panic attacks when they are anxious, accompanied by extremely shallow breathing, as well as other automatic bodily responses. Other symptoms of a panic attack are chest pains, heart palpitations, sweating, nausea, and dizziness.

Experiencing anxiety to this degree is at the severe end of the spectrum, and some people with NES experience panic attacks. However, if you do become anxious and stressed, paying attention to the way you breathe can help you to reduce the tension you feel. Decreasing this tension, in turn, can reduce your sleeping problems and your urge to eat in order to ease yourself back to sleep.

The following breathing exercises are particularly helpful to people suffering from the anxious/agitated type of NES and from the all-or-nothing belief about sleep. They will also be helpful to the other two types of NES.

Breathing to Relax

The alternative to shallow breathing with your chest muscles is breathing deeply with your abdominal muscles, also known as *diaphragmatic breathing*. Stop reading for a moment and observe how you are breathing right now. You're probably breathing more with your chest than your abdominal muscles. Think about how you breathe when you are very relaxed or sleeping. During those times, your breathing is slow and regular and sounds louder. These breaths are produced by your abdominal muscles. To test the difference between breathing from your chest and your abdominal muscles, do the following quick exercise.

Exercise: Breathing from Your Abdomen

1. To practice breathing from the muscles in your diaphragm, sit or lie down with your legs and arms uncrossed and your back straight.

2. Place your hand over your stomach and let out a laugh, similar to Santa's "Ho! Ho! Ho!" Can you feel where your laughter comes from?

3. If you let out a deep belly laugh, then your air is coming from the muscles in your diaphragm. This is where you want your deep, abdominal breathing to take place.

4. Make the transition from breathing with your chest muscles to breathing with your abdominal muscles by inhaling deeply while you count to yourself.

5. Count slowly, "1 . . . 2 . . . 3 . . . 4" as you inhale. Feel your chest and your stomach expand. At the end of your count, release your breath (exhale) slowly to the same count of 4. If you would rather use words to help calm yourself, you can substitute those words for the counting.

6. Continue repeating this exercise for five minutes. Notice how your muscles start to relax. As you concentrate on your breathing and counting, your mind will also clear, helping to distract you from the anxiety-provoking thoughts you were having and from thoughts about eating.

Practice this exercise during the day when you're not feeling anxious. Next, try using it when you feel your anxiety level rising. Finally try it when you feel anxious in the evening or when you awaken during the night. It is essential to feel comfortable using this breathing technique to calm yourself down, because, at first, it may not occur to you to try it at night. We've already suggested that you wait at least five minutes when you wake up at night before you decide whether you still want something to eat. While you are waiting for those five minutes to pass, try these deep-breathing exercises. Over time, this type of breathing should relax you significantly and help ease you back to sleep.

Progressive Muscle Relaxation

Another popular method for releasing tension is called *progressive muscle relaxation.* This method, along with deep breathing, will help you at those times when you are keyed up, especially in the middle of the night. Researchers at the University of South Carolina have shown that repeated use of progressive muscle relaxation is a helpful tool for treating NES (Pawlow, O'Neil, and Malcolm 2003). Often, when you are anxious and agitated, your muscles become tense and your body is unable to relax. This exercise focuses on releasing the tension in each muscle group throughout your body. By reducing the tension, you also lower your heart rate and blood pressure, and relaxation sets in.

Exercise: Progressive Muscle Relaxation—Part I

1. Begin by sitting or lying down on your back comfortably with your arms and legs uncrossed.

2. Close your eyes and breathe deeply to the count of four (as you practiced above). Practice tightening your muscles for five seconds and then relaxing them for twenty seconds.

3. Feel the contrast between the tensing and relaxing of your muscles. Remembering this feeling will allow you to assess your tension level during a stressful situation.

We will walk you through each muscle group once, but if you still feel tense after doing the exercise for any particular muscle group, repeat it for up to four or five times until you feel those tight muscles loosen.

Exercise: Progressive Muscle Relaxation—Part II

1. Start by clenching your fists. Hold this for five seconds. Notice the tension in your fingers, hands, and forearms. Then release. Relax for about twenty seconds. As noted above, you may need to repeat this part of the exercise as many as four or five times before you notice that these muscles are sufficiently relaxed.

2. Next, move the focus up your arms as you flex your biceps. Hold this position and feel the tension there. Then release and relax for twenty seconds.

3. Move your attention to your shoulders. The shoulders and neck are very common areas to hold onto tension. Shrug your shoulders up toward your ears and hold for five seconds. Release and relax. Repeat as necessary.

4. When you release, feel the tension leaving your neck and shoulders. Roll your head slowly to the left and the right to release any extra tension.

5. Continue by moving up to your head. Now, clench your jaws together for five seconds, and then release. Open and close your mouth several times, moving your tongue around. Make sure your entire lower face feels heavy and relaxed. Continue to think about tension leaving your body. Close your eyes tightly, and then release, all the while observing how relaxed your muscles feel as you release the tension. When you reach the top of your head, wrinkle your forehead. When you are satisfied that your shoulders, neck, and head are relaxed, move down to the trunk of your body.

6. To tighten your chest, take a breath in and hold it. Feel the tension being released as you breathe out. Do that several times. Then, move down your body to your stomach. Tense your abdominal muscles, then breathe out. Now take another deep breath and feel your abdomen expand. Hold and release. The final area of your trunk is your back. Arch your back, without straining, and hold. Try to keep your other muscles as loose as possible. Release.

7. Now, we move the focus to the lower body. Start with your buttocks. Practice tensing for five seconds and then relaxing for twenty seconds. Then move down to your thighs. After releasing the tension in these muscles, move down to concentrate on your calf muscles. Flex your calf muscles by pointing your toes, and release. Finally, you reach your feet. Flex your feet toward your knees. You will feel the tightness up the front of your shins. Release, and relax.

8. At this point your limbs should feel heavy and relaxed. Your tension will be lessened; if not completely gone. If you notice lingering tightness in any area, go back and tighten and release those muscles until you feel the heaviness of relaxation return.

Remember to do this exercise slowly. It should take you at least fifteen minutes if you do it correctly. Progressive muscle relaxation can easily be done in the middle of the night when you are feeling agitated and in need of comfort. Try to use this kind of relaxing comfort instead of the comfort that you get from eating your favorite nighttime snacks.

Areas to Target with Progressive Muscle Relaxation

- Fists—fingers, hands, and forearms
- Biceps
- Shoulders and neck
- Jaw
- Eyes
- Forehead
- Chest
- Stomach/abdomen
- Back
- Buttocks
- Thighs
- Calf muscles
- Feet

Factors That Influence Your Sleep

Not sleeping well is an unpleasant experience for anyone, and some people are especially sensitive to not getting enough sleep. We've all heard of people who seem to function just fine on four to five hours of sleep per night. But, as a rule, most people need seven to nine hours for their mind and body to stay healthy and to function at their best.

As mentioned in chapter 8, most night eaters seem to get the same total amount of sleep as people without NES. However, if you have NES, you have more frequent awakenings and lower sleep efficiency. Sleep efficiency is the ratio of the time you spend sleeping compared to the total amount of time between your bed-time and morning rise times (O'Reardon et al., Working paper 2004). We are still trying to discover why you are having these awakenings, especially those that occur within the first half of your sleeping time. Awakenings during this time are unusual; for you to be waking up an hour or two after going to sleep is a real problem.

Once you are up, especially if you hold the all-or-nothing belief about sleep, you may start to worry that you won't be able to fall back asleep. You may be convinced that you must eat something or you will never get back to sleep. Then you start having thoughts like, "I can't afford to lose another wink of sleep. If I don't fall back to sleep soon, I'll be sleepy all day tomorrow. I won't be able to do my presentation as well as I planned, and my boss will be disappointed in me." Thoughts like these are all-or-nothing beliefs because you think that either (1) you will sleep through the night and be able to function perfectly the next day (all), or (2) any amount of sleep you lose to awakenings will ruin the coming day (nothing).

Factors Associated with the Quality of Your Sleep

We have discussed several different strategies to address your eating. Now we turn our attention to the factors that affect your sleep. First, practicing the breathing and progressive muscle relaxation exercises should help in both relaxing you and helping you fall back to sleep. These techniques are often used to treat the usual kinds of insomnia. Second, your *sleep hygiene,* that is, your sleep-related habits, will affect your quality of sleep. Third, your beliefs about sleep are also an important influence on how well you are able to fall back to sleep after you awaken.

Sleep Hygiene and Faulty Beliefs

There are several things you can do to improve your sleep hygiene. First, try to relax and unwind before going to sleep. This may be accomplished by some simple stretching, breathing exercises, or even by reading a good book. Next, don't go to bed unless you are sleepy. This is especially true if you consistently have *initial insomnia,* trouble falling asleep for twenty to thirty minutes or more. It is also important not to *try* to fall asleep. Like the saying "A watched pot never boils," the more you think about falling asleep, the more it seems it will never happen.

One expert in treating insomnia offered some good insights into beliefs about sleep and how they can magnify the effects of your insomnia. Dr. Charles Morin (2001) recommends that you should keep realistic expectations about your sleep. For example, if you know that you wake up two to three times each night, accept the fact that, at first, you won't completely stop those awakenings, and understand that it will take some time and hard work to decrease them. Don't blame your awakenings and insomnia for all of your daytime problems. There are bound to be other factors that influence your level of functioning during the day, factors like your overall stress levels, your amount of social support, and how difficult the situation is that you are trying to tackle.

Morin also suggests that you should not give too much importance to sleep. If you focus too much of your attention on your problems with awakenings, your anxiety level will rise, making sleep even harder to maintain. Furthermore, you should try not to do what is called *catastrophizing* (making a big deal out of a situation and predicting terrible consequences from it) about the effects of a poor night's sleep. The more you worry about how you woke up the night before and what effects it will have on your day, the more likely it is that you will be negatively impacted. It is a kind of self-fulfilling prophecy.

Finally, you should try to develop a tolerance to the effects of your sleep loss. If you have been suffering with NES for a long time, you may have already tried to adapt your daytime functioning. This could mean trying to complete your most challenging work when you have the most energy—either the morning or evening, depending on how tired you feel. For others, unfortunately, this could mean drinking a dozen cups of coffee.

Caffeine and Other Substances Affecting Sleep

We have heard from many people with NES that they are big coffee drinkers. They often start their day with a few cups in the morning and drink other caffeinated drinks, like colas or iced tea, in the afternoon and even in the evening. (Don't forget, chocolate also contains caffeine, especially dark chocolate.) You may be drinking caffeine to combat the grogginess you feel from a poor night's sleep. However, you are reinforcing the cycle of insomnia if you drink this much caffeine, especially after the noon hour. Having more than two caffeinated beverages a day can worsen your problems with sleeping.

You have probably heard some horror stories about individuals trying to quit using a drug, whether illegal, such as cocaine or heroin, or readily available, such as alcohol or cigarettes. Well, it's important to remember that caffeine is a drug, too. And, just as people encounter problems when trying to stop using other drugs, you, too, may have difficulty cutting back on your caffeine intake and experience symptoms of caffeine withdrawal. These include headaches, irritability, jitters, and even some depression. You might also have a rebound, where at first your sleep problems worsen. Therefore, you should try to withdraw from caffeine slowly, over a period of a few weeks, depending on how much you have been drinking when you start to cut down.

Similarly, smoking cigarettes also interferes with sleeping. Nicotine, like caffeine, is a stimulant, and many smokers complain of insomnia. Cutting down, or preferably, quitting smoking entirely, will help you to fall asleep faster and decrease the number of times that you awaken during the night.

Finally, although you may feel the relaxing effects of alcohol while you are awake, it can actually disrupt your sleeping patterns. If you have had a few drinks within a couple of hours of your bedtime, you may have found that you were able to fall asleep more easily. However, the *quality* of your sleep will be worse. You won't be getting as much deep sleep, and you will have more awakenings, although they may be brief.

As with caffeine consumption, if you are drinking alcohol at night, cut down on the amount you drink. Do it gradually over the course of a couple of weeks. After a month, you should find that the quality of your sleep has improved.

This Chapter's Goals

- Continue to keep your food journal. Gradually introduce a healthy breakfast and structured meal and snack times into your schedule.

- Designate an area in your home that is the only place where you allow yourself to eat. This will limit mindless snacking while watching TV or sitting in front of the computer.

- Using the exposure method, try introducing some of your forbidden foods to your diet. When you are comfortable with this during the day, try using the same method at night.

- Practice the imagery exercises during the day, and as you begin to feel comfortable with them, use them at night to reinforce the reasons why you shouldn't eat.

- Practice the breathing and progressive muscle relaxation techniques. These can be used together with the imagery exercises to resist your compulsions to eat.

- Examine your sleep hygiene and practice the tips provided. Cut down on caffeine, alcohol, and smoking.

- Remember to do all of these things gradually. Make long-term lifestyle changes, not changes that just last a week!

CHAPTER 10

I'll Get By with a Little Help from My Friends

By now, we hope you've tried some of the exercises suggested in earlier chapters to overcome your night eating. If you have, this means that you may have tried to eat more regular meals during the day, and to keep track of your thoughts and emotions when you are eating at night. You may also have tried some of the stress-reduction exercises, such as diaphragmatic breathing and progressive muscle relaxation. Although you can perform most of these exercises and activities as an individual, remember you have others out there to help you. Don't forget that social support from family, friends, and others will also help you to overcome your night eating. In this chapter, we'll highlight some of the ways that social support can come in handy, and we'll tell you how you can help others who may have NES.

Reaching Out to Others

The first step in getting support from others is reaching out to them, letting them know you want help. If you have the tendency to keep your night eating a secret, this could have come about for many reasons. You may be embarrassed by it, or you may think that others might not understand. You may have told someone about your problem in the past, only to receive unhelpful comments in response. Have you heard, or even imagined, people saying things like, "Well, just don't get up and eat," or "You must have no willpower." Listening to feedback like this when you are trying to get support can be discouraging and frustrating.

Opening up an honest dialogue with a friend, significant other, or family member can help you *and* them get past such superficial comments that are meant to help, even if they are misguided. Sitting down with someone and talking about your struggle with night eating takes courage. If you know someone who you think would be supportive of your efforts to end your night eating, then summoning the courage to hold this conversation will be worth your while. How do you go about opening an honest dialogue?

First, pick a time to talk to a supportive person (or people) when there will be few interruptions. Second, pick a place to talk that will be comfortable for you. You may feel comfortable talking to someone at a crowded mall or restaurant, while someone else may feel more comfortable in a quiet room at home. Setting up the right time and place will help ensure that the person you choose to trust will be able to devote full attention to you. It will also ensure that you will have enough time to explain the full impact of your night eating and how he or she could be helpful with your goal of overcoming this condition. (Note: For the purpose of the remainder of this discussion we will assume your friend is a girl or woman. We understand that your friend may be male, but we are choosing to make the text easier to read.)

What Do You Say Now?

When you have your supportive friend's attention, what do you say? Everyone has a personal style of communicating. It could be comical or serious. Whatever it is, you should approach the topic in a way that is most comfortable for you. The person you choose to talk to might even be aware of your night eating but she may have thought it was an off-limits topic, one that wasn't polite to discuss with you. Your friend may feel relieved that you brought up the topic so that she can learn how to help you. There may be people who know of your late night trips to the kitchen, but they may have been discouraged from helping before because you didn't appear to be receptive to their help in the past. They may really want to know what they can do, so they, too, can help.

When telling your friend about your struggles with NES, let her know that you are trying to change your eating habits and patterns. You also may want to share how frustrating and distressing NES has been for you. It's important to get across the point that NES is not simply a bad habit. It is a syndrome that many people struggle with in secret; it's not something that can be changed in the blink of an eye. Once your friends understand how hard it is for you to live with NES, and they recognize how hard it may have been for you to disclose such personal information, it is likely that they will wish to do whatever they can to help you.

What Can Others Do to Help?

There are two types of support that you can receive from your friend: emotional and instrumental. If your friend does not live with you, then most of the support will be emotional. However, if the person you have shared with does live with you, you are likely to receive both emotional and instrumental support.

Emotional support can take different forms. It could mean that someone just takes the time to listen to your efforts at changing your night eating. It could also mean that you have someone to check in with each day about your efforts during the previous night. It's possible that your friend may start asking too many questions for your taste, or become too overbearing. If that happens, talk with her about what kind of support you need and want. Some people like having to be accountable to someone, while others may see this as someone looking over their shoulder. Only you will know what kind of support will be most helpful to you.

Instrumental support (also called *behavioral support*) can come from the people who live with you. There are several instrumental strategies that can supplement your work with stimulus control and changing your automatic thoughts. Some of the more helpful strategies include putting all tempting foods in a place that's hard to reach, such as a car or basement. Your support person can not only make sure that these foods are moved to this place each night but can and motivate you to keep up your efforts.

Another way to keep your foods out of reach is to lock your refrigerator or cabinets. If you find yourself unlocking the cabinets during the night, you can ask your support person to hold or hide the key or use a combination lock with a code that you don't know. After a while, you should have a better handle on your cravings and how to temper them, as you learned through the work you did in chapters 8 and 9. When that happens, you can experiment with unlocking your refrigerator or food cabinets again.

Other patients have described using alarms to stop their nighttime eating. Some people activate their security alarms so that they will ring if they go into the kitchen. Others install a door chime or an alarm that you can find at your local hardware store. These either ring or set off an alarm when you open your bedroom door—or whatever door on which you choose to install it. Your spouse or housemate should keep the code so that you aren't tempted to get up and turn it off to get to the kitchen. After it is installed, if you try getting into the kitchen without the code, then you would set off the alarm and wake up your family or housemates—or even the neighbors!

Some of these strategies sound extreme, but if your night eating is very distressing, you may need such barriers and obstacles. In such a case, the help of others can make all the difference in whether these strategies work or not. These radical measures may cause you some stress. If so, this would be a good time to try some of the relaxation and breathing exercises instead of going to the kitchen. However, if you really want to decrease your night eating, trying something extreme may be the key to getting you started and keeping you on your road to recovery.

What Others Can Say in the Middle of the Night

It's all well and good to talk to your support person and receive emotional support during the day. But daytime is not the problem, is it? No. It's during the night when you need the most support to help you change. What can you do about that? One good idea would be to talk to your friend during the day to figure out what will be most helpful in the middle of the night. What can someone say to you? If you get agitated when you are up in the middle of the night, then you may want to tell your friend to be patient with you while you are adjusting to becoming more receptive about receiving help. The more you talk about your night eating with your friend during the day, the more aware you will be during the night that this person is trying to help you.

About a hundred years ago, a man named Emile Coué had an enormous impact on the mental health movement in America and abroad. His major tool was a mantra. A *mantra* is a word or phrase that you find comforting and reinforcing. For many years, numbers of Americans were fervent advocates of Coué and his mantra, which was "Day by day in every way I am getting better and better." Today Coué is looked upon as an interesting historical figure, and his movement has vanished. But at the time, his mantra was a major fixture in American society. If you think that this mantra would help you, feel free to adopt it and tell your support person about it. Otherwise, find a short phrase that you can make your own. A mantra may be able to help you control your night eating.

For example, you can repeat your chosen phrase to yourself, one such as, "I am not hungry. I will go back to sleep." Work on those words that would provide you with the most comfort and help when the going gets tough. You can repeat your mantra as you do your breathing exercises, and the two can reinforce each other. You can also tell your chosen mantra to your housemate. When you are up at night looking for food and not using your mantra, your housemate can repeat your mantra out loud to help coax you back to bed. The more you believe in what you are saying, the more effective the words will be, and the more you will be able to identify with them when you are reminded of them in the middle of the night

Your support person could also talk to you about something that is meaningful to you. Perhaps you have a social function coming up and you are trying to lose a few pounds. You could ask your housemate to remind you of this event when you are trying to get up out of bed to eat, or when you are snacking before you go to bed. Again, if your friend tells you this in a way that is too invasive or overbearing, you may suggest a better way of saying it, or not saying it at all. However, this external support may be the just the extra motivation you need to implement the strategies explained in earlier chapters.

You Might Run across Other Night Eaters

The more you reach out and tell your friends and family about your NES, the more likely you are to find others who have NES, or who know someone else who has it. This may provide a golden opportunity for you to team up with another night eater. Working together to help each other stay on track and sharing and exchanging helpful strategies for reducing night eating will be positively reinforcing and may give you more hope for change.

As discussed in chapter 6, NES seems to be genetically driven in some cases. This means you may even discover a family member who has NES and who has been suffering alone. Some of our patients recall running into their mother or father at the refrigerator in the middle of the night. Others say that they remember from their childhood seeing (or hearing) a parent or a grandparent up and about and eating at night. Because NES was discussed even less in the past than it is today, any relatives who have the problem may be relieved to have someone like you to talk to about it.

Some people have no reservations about talking to family and friends about their struggles. Others, however, do not feel as comfortable. Some families are very strict about keeping their problems secret. If that has been the case in your family, you may feel that no one in your family wants to help you. But, there is help from outside the family, as we have discussed; also you may be able to find help on the Internet.

An Internet listserv called "Nightgrazers" has a large membership. Members share their struggles and successes on a daily basis. Many have found comfort in this personal, yet anonymous, connection. They are dedicated to finding a way to change their eating patterns, as well as to accept that they suffer from a syndrome—one with which it is very hard to cope. There are members from across the Unites States and Canada, as well as from Great Britain, and other points abroad. To join, send an e-mail introducing yourself to the following address: Night grazerssubscribe@yahoogroups.co.uk. The group moderator will get you started. You can write to them as little or as much as you are comfortable with, but the people who choose to participate more seem to get the most out of the experience.

Health Care Providers and NES

After reaching this point in the book, you should know much more about NES than when you read chapter 1, where we first touched upon talking to your physician. Now that you are armed with more information, hopefully you can explain more effectively to your physician how you are affected by NES. For example, lack of sleep may be your main concern, and you may suspect that you have a sleep disorder in addition to NES, like those described in chapter 5. In that case, tell your doctor about the symptoms you have noticed. Also report what your sleeping partner (if you have one) has observed about your sleeping habits. This may include loud snoring, gasping for air, jerking of your legs or arms, or violent night terrors. Being able to report these problems will allow your doctor to make appropriate diagnoses and perhaps to give you a referral to a sleep specialist.

If you do not have symptoms of other sleep disorders, but you are overweight or obese, talk to your physician about the impact your NES is having on your weight. This will give him or her more insight into why it has been so difficult to lose some of the weight that is adversely affecting your health. If you haven't told your physician about your night eating, he or she may think that you haven't tried to follow the weight loss recommendations that were given to you at past visits. (See chapter 1 for a discussion of disorders related to overweight and obesity.) Be sure to be clear about the efforts you've already put forth.

Mental Health Care Providers

You may want to seek counseling or therapy for your NES, particularly if you have a high level of stress, depression, anxiety, or just general distress. Unfortunately, at this point in time, not many mental health professionals know much about NES. If you have a therapist or counselor, sharing this book with him or her might be a good start. If you don't know of a therapist or counselor and think that you may need one, ask your primary care physician for a referral. Another option could be to see whether there are any therapists or psychiatrists who specialize in eating or weight disorders in your area.

The therapeutic approach we present in this book is called *cognitive behavioral*, but other approaches, such as *interpersonal psychotherapy* or *psychodynamic psychotherapy* may also be helpful. Although each therapist has unique approaches to helping patients, cognitive behavioral therapy deals more with the here and now and the patient's inner dialogue.

Interpersonal and psychodynamic therapies, on the other hand, frequently delve into your past and help you to think deeply about your family and relationship situations. Ask the therapist to explain her or his preferred theoretical approach before you begin treatment. In that way, you'll understand more about the issues that you'll be exploring in therapy. This explanation and your feelings about the therapist will help you to decide whether this professional is the right match for you.

Today, many therapists describe their approach as *eclectic*, meaning that they use different strategies from the many schools of thought in psychology, and they apply them as they see fit, depending on the problems that are presented. When looking for a therapist, the key is to find someone with whom you feel comfortable. After all, you'll be discussing personal matters with this person. You should trust that he or she will be empathic and helpful, no matter what you have to say. As with the listserv we mentioned above, the more effort you put into therapy, the more you get out of it.

If you're wondering about the different types of mental health care providers, here is a brief description. Basically there are three kinds, and each has distinctive features. Psychiatrists have a medical degree (M.D.) in addition to other schooling in mental health. They can prescribe medications. Some also conduct psychotherapy, while others work in conjunction with a nonmedical therapist. Psychologists have a doctor of philosophy degree (Ph.D.) or a doctor of psychology degree (Psy.D.). Both types of psychologists have extensive training in psychotherapy. Ph.D.'s usually have more training in research than those with Psy.D. degrees, who usually receive more clinical training in graduate school. However, both can provide psychotherapy and psychological testing. At this point in time, psychologists cannot prescribe medications, although a movement is underway to change this.

Social workers (MSWs) and family and child counselors (MFCCs) usually have a master's degree and have been trained specifically for counseling. If nonmedical therapists feel that medication would be helpful, they usually work with a psychiatrist.

Any of these professionals can be helpful to you. You should feel that you have a good fit with your therapist, and it is important that he or she is open to learning more about NES. If you do not feel comfortable with the first person that you see, don't be discouraged. Look for someone else. If you live in a city, you will have more choices than if you live in a small town. But, even if your options are limited (or if you feel you aren't getting your needs met), seek out someone else.

This Chapter's Goals

- Pick someone to talk to about your NES. Arrange for a comfortable setting and a protected time to talk to this person.

- Decide how you want your friends or housemates to help you: emotionally, instrumentally, or both.

- Consider whether you would like to seek counseling or therapy to help you with your night eating. If you do, talk to your health care provider about a referral.

CHAPTER 11

Take Two Pills and Call
Me in the Morning

You are now nearing the end of our book. We hope that you have faithfully carried out our many recommendations, such as keeping a food diary and keeping track of your thoughts in your journal about your night eating. Despite all of your efforts, you still may have some of the symptoms of NES. You may be discouraged; you may even be thinking of throwing in the towel and giving up. Wait! There is still another avenue to explore in your struggle against NES.

Although we've stressed behavioral approaches to overcoming NES, we also recognize that certain medications may be helpful for treating NES. The research on these medications and their role in controlling night eating is still in its early stages. We will review what we know about these medical treatments and describe what our patients have told us about their experiences with medications before coming to us.

Treatments: Trial and Error?

When working with night eaters, one of the first things we asked our patients was to tell us what prescription medications and over-the-counter remedies they had tried to control their NES. Then, we made a list of all the things they'd tried, and went over it very carefully. Even though quite an array of medications had been taken, the striking finding was that almost nothing worked. A few medications helped some of the people some of the time, but nothing worked consistently. There was one exception, the medication combination called fen-phen.

Fen-Phen

You probably recall the publicity about the wonder drug combination of two medications, fenfluramine and phentermine, for the treatment of obesity in the early 1990s. This treatment had great success in helping people lose weight. Those of our patients who had tried this combination reported that their night eating disappeared while they were taking these medications. Unfortunately, it turned out that the long-term use of these drugs caused heart valve problems, and fen-phen was taken off the market.

The experience with fen-phen was important in helping us understand what may control night eating. This combination produced a very large increase in the neurotransmitter *serotonin* in the areas of the brain that deal with appetite. This knowledge helped direct attention to medications that might help in the treatment of NES, particularly those medications that affect serotonin.

Over-the-Counter Medications

Over-the-counter remedies have been widely used by night eaters, but they have shown very little benefit. Two of the most common treatments are the hormone melatonin and an herbal medication made from the kava kava root. Some patients reported that these two agents helped them fall asleep, but they didn't stay asleep. In fact, they told us that they still woke up during the night and ate.

All of these reports were anecdotal, and we don't know how many night eaters have tried these remedies. If you are going to try any over-the-counter medications or herbal preparations for any condition, be sure to consult your physician first. This is important, especially if you are taking other medications.

Sleeping Pills

You may have tried sleeping pills. After all, it seems reasonable: when you have trouble sleeping, sleeping pills should help you get to sleep and stay asleep. However, when we looked at the reports from our patients, one of the most striking results was how ineffective sleeping pills were for treating NES. Although they may help some people to fall asleep, unfortunately they have little or no effect on nocturnal awakenings. So, if you've been discouraged because sleeping pills haven't helped you, take heart. They haven't helped other night eaters, either.

We've recently found a reason for the ineffectiveness of sleeping medication. Although we've discussed the complexity of NES and some other disorders that share some similar symptoms, such as depression and sleep apnea (see chapter 5), night eating syndrome is primarily an eating disorder, not a sleeping disorder. The problems with sleeping are caused by the problems with the urge to eat, and not because there is anything wrong with the basic sleep mechanism, as discussed in chapter 3. There have been reports that some people with NS-RED, the sleepwalking type of night eating discussed in chapter 5, have been helped by sleeping pills. However, people with NES tell us that sleeping pills, both prescription, such as zolpidem (Ambien), and over-the-counter sleep aids do help them *fall* asleep. But, as with herbal and hormonal remedies, this doesn't prevent them from waking up and getting out of bed to eat.

In fact, sleeping pills may make it more difficult to control your night eating. Patients say that when they are under the influence of sleeping pills, their level of awareness of their eating is much less than usual; they also say that they feel they exercise less control over what and how much they eat. Some patients who had never before experienced sleepwalking and eating reported not remembering their eating episodes when taking sleeping pills. The only way they knew they had been up and eating was by finding evidence of the activity, such as crumbs and wrappers in the kitchen or in their beds, the next morning. Therefore, even if falling asleep is a major problem, steer clear of sleeping pills. They actually may work against your efforts at controlling your night eating.

Selective Serotonin Reuptake Inhibitors

Unfortunately, medication, alone or in combination, has had little success either with weight loss or with NES. We mentioned that the effect of fen-phen was to increase the levels of the neurotransmitter serotonin in the brain areas controlling appetite. It seemed logical then that selective serotonin reuptake inhibitors (SSRIs) would have similar results. Under their personal physicians' care, several patients tried various SSRIs. You may be familiar with some of their names, such as fluoxetine (Prozac), sertraline (Zoloft), and paroxetine (Paxil). These medications were originally designed for the treatment of depression.

Recently, however, they have been approved for other problems, such as anxiety disorders and eating disorders. Their efficacy in conditions other than depression and the experience with fen-phen suggested that we try the SSRI sertraline (Zoloft).

A Treatment Study of NES

Our NES research team at the University of Pennsylvania enrolled seventeen patients into an *open-label trial* of sertraline, in which its effectiveness was not compared with a *placebo* (sugar pill). For this reason, patients' responses may be due, in part, to the suggestion of taking a medication, also known as the *placebo effect*. As a result, the outcome of an open-label trial may seem stronger and more favorable than that of a trial with a placebo, which is why the Food and Drug Administration (FDA) requires new medications to be tested in comparison with a placebo. For twelve weeks, the patients took sertraline under our team's supervision. They visited our offices every two weeks to assess their progress and to increase the amount of sertraline they were taking if it was not decreasing their symptoms.

We found that, at the end of the twelve weeks, there was significant improvement in each of our four primary measures. Total nighttime awakenings dropped by more than 50 percent, and awakenings with snacking were reduced by two-thirds. The total number of calories that patients ate after supper also fell by 50 percent. The ratings of overall improvement in NES symptoms, as judged by the patient and doctor together, also significantly improved.

The four patients who improved the most lost a significant amount of weight, but those who did not experience as much relief for their symptoms lost no weight. Thus, those who responded best to the effects of sertraline had two very favorable outcomes: control of their night eating and weight loss. Five patients could not tolerate sertraline and dropped out of the study before the completion of the twelve weeks. They complained of either feeling sedated or feeling anxious, even at low doses of the medication.

Depression decreased on average among participants, as would be expected with an antidepressant such as sertraline. However, the improvement in NES symptoms does not appear to be simply the result of our patients' moods improving. Whether patients had a high level of depression before the study or not, they were just as likely to find relief from NES.

What Do These Findings Mean for You?

In view of the good outcome with sertraline in the study we just described, it is surprising that some patients had reported receiving SSRIs from their own doctors with little or no benefit. The reason may be that they received an inadequate dose of medication, failed to take it regularly, or didn't receive it for a long enough time. There is no magic pill for NES, but researchers are looking for more options.

Future Medication Options

The initial success of sertraline that we've reported gives us the hope that the pharmaceutical industry will try to develop medication specifically for NES. As NES becomes more widely recognized, these attempts will increase. Stay tuned for more research on sertraline and other medications and their effects on NES, as more and more researchers are becoming interested in finding effective treatments for this syndrome.

This Chapter's Goals

- If you are interested in trying sertraline to control your night eating, talk to your doctor. If she or he is not familiar with NES, asking her or him to read this chapter would be a good place to start.

- If you and your doctor decide to start a trial of sertraline, ask her or him to read the paper by O'Reardon, Stunkard, and Allison in the *International Journal of Eating Disorders* (in press) and/or to get in touch with our research team at the University of Pennsylvania's Weight and Eating Disorders Program (215-898-7314) for advice.

PART IV

Don't Give Up!

This final chapter sums up how NES can affect you and how you can recover from NES. It also cautions against some pitfalls that you may encounter along the way and tells you how to stay on track on your road to recovery.

CHAPTER 12

Final Thoughts and Encouragement

Congratulations! You made it through to the end. We recognize that, like some of us, you may be the kind of person who jumps to the last chapter to see how the book ends. If so, be sure you take the time to read through the whole book to get the most benefit from each chapter. If you are hoping to change your NES, then it is essential to do the exercises that appear in many chapters.

On the other hand, if you have been reading the book thoroughly, chapter by chapter, and faithfully doing the exercises, you probably have made strides toward curbing your night eating. No matter where you are in your recovery, hopefully you've learned a great deal about the different aspects of NES, and you've gained some insight into your difficulties in dealing with it.

Some Take-Home Messages

By this point you should know that NES affects many different kinds of people: both men and women and all races and ethnicities. It mainly affects adults but, occasionally, it can start in childhood or adolescence. We also know that NES exists in many different countries; it is not just a North American phenomenon.

So, don't feel that you are suffering alone. There are others out there with the same problems.

It is also important to remember that NES affects people in different ways. For example, you may have no appetite in the morning and overeat before you go to bed, but not wake up at night. Or, you might overeat before you go to bed and also eat when you wake during the night. You may suffer from a mild depression most of the time, while someone else may not have many difficulties with his or her moods. The main aspect of NES that you, as a night eater, share with other night eaters is the shift in the pattern of your food intake. Although the symptoms may vary from person to person, you all experience a delay in your food intake so that you eat less in the morning and more than average amounts of food each evening and night.

Because no two people's experience with NES is identical, we are continuing to work on defining the different types of night eating. The four that we've identified so far are described in chapter 8. These types are the compelled evening and nighttime overeater, the anxious/agitated night eater, the cravings night eater, and the all-or-nothing belief about sleep night eater. You may identify specifically with one or more types, or you may have experienced the thoughts associated with each type at different times. We've described some techniques that will target these thoughts and your subsequent actions—nighttime eating—that will work for each type.

Reinforcing the Change Strategies

While you may get a great deal of insight into NES from just reading this book, insight will not help you control your night eating. You must try to use the strategies that have been outlined. This will take time and effort. Changing your lifestyle, whether trying to lose weight or trying to shift your pattern of night eating, can be a long journey. You must be willing to push yourself and stick with the changes you make to your daily routines in order to control your night eating.

Keeping a food and thought journal, as discussed in chapters 2 and 8, can be a helpful and useful tool for changing your eating habits. Health practitioners who specialize in weight loss know that most people think that they know how many calories they consume on a daily basis. But until they begin to write down exactly what they are eating throughout the day, including little snacks or pieces of candy here and there, they tend to under-estimate their total caloric intake for each day. Only by paying careful attention to what they actually eat can they truly hit their target calorie range and begin to lose weight.

Such is the case with night eating, as well. Until you force yourself to examine what you actually eat and the thoughts you actually have both before and after you eat, you may not under-stand all of the ways that this syndrome is affecting you—both physically and emotionally. Therefore, no matter how tiresome or difficult it may seem to write down a record of all the food you consume and all the thoughts you have about your eating in your journal, this is the one aspect of this program that is essential for your recovery. We can't stress this point enough. Keep your food and thoughts journal consistently and carefully updated.

The other techniques explained within the book are also very important. Once you have a good idea about the pattern of your food intake and the types of thoughts that you are having, you can then try to resist your usual eating patterns. Use the help of the imagery, breathing, and progressive muscle relaxation exer-cises that you've learned. Enlisting the help of trusted friends and family will also give you support to reach your goals. They may provide you with words of encouragement or physical help with limiting your access to food at night in any number of different ways.

Accepting Relapses

You've worked so hard to get your night eating under control. And then you slipped. You started eating at night again. This is not a rare experience. A great many people experience the occasional setback, or lapse, in their improved eating habits. Be prepared for these relapses when they occur, accept them, learn from them, and get back into your new routines.

How do you think you will deal with a setback? It's an excellent idea to plan ahead, before it happens. It will be vital for you to remember that an occasional bad night or two is not the same thing as falling off the wagon and having a complete relapse. The way you think about one or two nights of eating—whether you view them as a small setback or a total relapse—is the key for determining how you will react. If you think of your bad night as a temporary setback, then you are better positioned to recover from it, and you can work that much harder to keep it from happening again.

If, on the other hand, you think of one or two nights of eating as a complete failure, then you will be more likely to say to yourself, "All this work was for nothing! No matter what I do, I can't beat this. I might as well give in and just eat what I want, when I want it." Once thoughts like these take effect, your efforts at making small but steady changes will have been wasted, and your night eating is likely to return in full force.

So, what should you do when you have had a difficult night? *Learn from it.* First, examine what else was going on for you at the time. Did you have a particularly stressful day? Was there a favorite food of yours in the house that you hadn't had in a while? Was your spouse or support person out of the house for the night? There could be many reasons, or combinations of circumstances, that contribute to a temporary setback. Take a few minutes to consider what these circumstances were, and write about them in your journal.

Raising your awareness about what triggered your difficult night will help you in the future when those same circumstances are present again. If you are aware of the reasons that contribute to your setbacks, then you can be better prepared to alert a supportive friend that you need help, or to take other steps against eating at night.

If you are confident that you have your night eating under control, we are very excited for you. However, even you may have a setback, and it is best to be prepared for it in advance. Not only is it wise to examine what the circumstances were that contributed to a bad night, it's also a good preventive measure to examine your journal from time to time to remind yourself of situations that may trigger night eating episodes in the future.

Expectations

Setting your expectations too high by thinking that you will never have another late-night snack will probably leave you feeling worse if a setback does occur than it would if you had prepared for that possibility. The reason it's unwise to set your expectations too high is that, if you feel as if you've suddenly failed, then you are more likely to view your behavior as a total relapse than if you were prepared for a slip-up from time to time.

Researching Your NES

We've provided you with a broad overview of the various aspects of the disorder that we've discovered up to the present. Now it's up to you to learn about your own NES in greater detail. In that sense, the more you try to learn about NES, the more you will become a researcher of your own syndrome, and the more you will come to learn from your own behaviors. Knowledge is a powerful tool. The more you understand about NES, the more seriously others may take you, whether it is the physician whom you ask for help or a friend whom you ask for support.

Many of the topics we covered are still in the early stages of research. We've provided you with the most up-to-date information we have on hormones, sleep (as it relates to NES), and how your emotions can impact on and are impacted by NES. However, you probably realized that, sadly, we don't yet have a complete answer as to how all of these functions cause and perpetuate NES.

We will continue our research, and NES is also becoming an area of increasing interest in the medical world. So, continue to keep an eye out for more information. The Internet is a good place to look for this type of information. Search engines and sites, such as www.google.com, www.yahoo.com, and www.webmd.com can provide you with links to current press releases on medical research. These press releases often mention the name of the journal in which the findings were published. If you live near a university or can access the particular journal online, you can keep yourself updated on the latest findings about NES. If you don't have this kind of access, you can also write to the authors of the research and ask them to send you a copy. As the scientific community learns more about NES, the more the word will spread to the media, increasing the amount of information available to the general public. Pieces of the complicated puzzle we call NES will surely come together in time.

Wrapping Up

Good luck with your efforts at controlling your night eating. If you have been faithful in carrying out the steps and exercises throughout this book, hopefully you've already realized some progress. Try not to forget that just as one size does not fit all, one approach does not work for everyone. So hang in there as you go through the good nights and bad nights you are bound to experience. Please try to enlist help from others to find the social support that you need. Our patients agree that this is an invaluable tool in their struggle to conquer NES.

When it seems that the stress of your daily grind is too much to handle, and you are ready to surrender again to your compulsion to eat at night, talk to someone, exercise, listen to music, treat yourself to a bubble bath, or get involved in another distracting activity. If you are consistently feeling overwhelmed, it may be time for you to seek counseling or therapy. If you do resume your eating for a night or two, don't beat yourself up. But do continue to fight NES using all of the techniques we've explored and discussed.

May your nights be filled with sleep and your days with healthy eating!

Appendix

Calculate Your Body Mass Index (BMI)

BMI = (weight in pounds multiplied by 703) divided by (height in inches multiplied by height in inches).

For example: If a woman weighs 200 pounds at 5 foot 4, to calculate her BMI, she must first convert her height into inches. Thus 5 foot 4 = 64 inches.

Then, she would insert her height and weight into the equation above, as shown here:

(200 x 703) divided by (64 x 64) = 140,600 divided by 4,096 = 34.3.

That number, 34.3, is the woman's BMI.

The National Institutes of Health have currently classified BMI as follows:

Below 18.5 = underweight

18.5 to 24.9 = normal weight

25 to 29.9 = overweight

30 or greater = obese

Clearly the woman is in the obese category. Night eating syndrome and the stressors in her life have really affected her over the years.

Muscle versus Fat

Although BMI is a relatively easy tool to use, it has limitations because it does not take into consideration the proportion of weight due to muscle versus the proportion due to fat.

If you exercise frequently by lifting weights or with consistent aerobic activity, your percentage of body fat may be low. Because muscle weighs more than fat, your BMI may overestimate the amount of fat in your body.

On the other hand, if you do not exercise regularly, your percentage of body fat could be high, and your BMI may underestimate the amount of fat in your body. On the whole, however, BMI is a good basic tool. Whether or not your BMI indicates that you are overweight or obese, you should work with your health care provider to maintain your optimal weight for optimal health.

Resources

Weight and Eating Disorders Organizations

Academy for Eating Disorders

www.aedweb.org: The academy is an international organization with members from the research and clinical community. They publish the *International Journal of Eating Disorders*, a journal that has been open to publishing research on NES.

Anorexia Nervosa and Related Eating Disorders, Inc.

www.anred.com: ANRED is a not-for-profit organization that has included the definition for NES on their Web site. They provide information to the public about many aspects of eating and weight disorders.

North American Association for the Study of Obesity

www.naaso.org: This organization publishes the journal *Obesity Research* and has shown interest in including research concerning NES. The Web site provides helpful information about obesity and related problems.

National Eating Disorders Association

www.nationaleatingdisorders.org: This site mainly deals with traditional eating disorders. The main focus is prevention and how to help others who may be affected.

Eating Right

American Dietetic Association

www.eatright.org: This is the site of the American Dietetic Association. It gives helpful hints about Dietary Reference Intakes (DRIs) at www.eatright.org/feature.1002.html.

Calorie Counter Resources

www.calorieking.com: This site is overseen by a clinical dietitian and includes a food database for calorie counting and nutritional content, as well as a free electronic food and exercise diary.

Bourushek, A. 2001. *The Doctor's Pocket Calorie, Fat & Carbohydrate Counter*. Costa Mesa, CA: Family Health Publications.

United States Department of Agriculture, Center for Nutrition Policy and Promotion

www.usda.gov/cnpp: This site has information about healthy diets. It also has a program for you to evaluate the nutritional content of your diet.

Promoting Good Sleep

The National Sleep Foundation

www.sleepfoundation.org: This site provides information about problems with sleeping and has an easy-to-use guide to sleep services nationwide.

National Center on Sleep Disorders Research Web site

www.nhlbi.nih.gov/about/ncsdr/: This site will provide you with information about ongoing research into sleep disorders. It also lists resources for the public.

Book

Hauri, P., and S. Linde. 1996. *No More Sleepless Nights* (rev. ed.). New York: John Wiley & Sons.

Morin, C. M., and C. A. Espic (Eds.) (2003). *Insomnia: A Clinical Guide to Assessment and Treatment*. New York: Kluwer Academic/Plenum Publishers.

Listserv for Night Eaters

Nightgrazers

Send an e-mail to Nightgrazers-subscribe@yahoogroups.co.uk. This listserv has members who suffer from NES from the United States as well as many other countries. They provide support and share information with each other about NES.

References

Adami, G. F., A. Meneghelli, and N. Scopinaro. 1999. Night eating and binge eating disorder in obese patients. *International Journal of Eating Disorders* 25:335-338.

Adler, G. K., B. T. Kinsley, S. Hurwitz, C. J. Mossey, and D. L. Goldenberg. 1999. Reduced hypothalamic-pituitary and sympathoadrenal responses to hypoglycemia in women with fibromyalgia syndrome. *American Journal of Medicine* 106: 534-543.

Allison, K. C., J. P. O'Reardon, D. F. Dinges, and A. J. Stunkard. 2004. Clinical characteristics of the night eating syndrome: Findings from a controlled study. Working paper, University of Pennsylvania, School of Medicine, Department of Psychiatry at Philadelphia.

Aronoff, N. J., A. Gliebter, S. A. Hashim, and G. K. Zammit. 1994. The relationship between daytime and nighttime food intake in an obese night-eater. *Obesity Research* 2:145-151.

Birketvedt, G. S., J. Florholmen, J. Sundsfjord, G. Osterud, D. Dinges, W. Bilker, et al. 1999. Behavioral and neuroendocrine characteristics of the night-eating syndrome. *Journal of the American Medical Association* 282:657-663.

Birketvedt, G. S., J. Sundsfjord, and J. R. Florholmen. 2002. Hypothalamic-pituitary-adrenal axis in the night eating syndrome.

American Journal of Physiology: Endocrinology and Metabolism 282:E366-E369.

Calle, E. E., C. Rodriguez, K. Walker-Thurmond, M. J. Thun. 2003. Overweight, obesity, and mortality from cancer in a prospectively studied cohort of U.S. adults. *New England Journal of Medicine* 348:1625-1638.

Cummings, D., D. Weigle, R. S. Frayo, P. A. Breen, M. K. Ma, E. P. Dellinger, et al. 2002. Plasma ghrelin levels after diet-induced weight loss or gastric bypass surgery. *New England Journal of Medicine* 345:1623-1630.

Dietary Reference Intakes: Applications in Dietary Assessment. 2001. Food and Nutrition Board. Institute of Medicine. National Academy Press: Washington DC.

Dinges, D. F., K. C. Allison, J. P. O'Reardon, N. Rogers, and A. J. Stunkard. 2003. Unpublished observations. Sleep characteristics of the night eating syndrome: A polysomnographic study.

DSM-IV-TR (Diagnostic and Statistical Manual of Mental Disorders, fourth edition, text revised). 2000. American Psychiatric Association: Washington, DC.

Epel, E. S., B. McEwen, T. Seeman, K. Matthews, G. Castellazzo, K. D. Brownell, et al. 2000. Stress and body shape: Stress-induced cortisol secretion is consistently greater among women with central fat. *Psychosomatic Medicine* 62:623-632.

Flegal, K. M., M. D. Carroll, C. L. Ogden, and C. L. Clifford. 2002. Prevalence trends in obesity among U.S. adults. *Journal of the American Medical Association* 288:1723-1727.

Foster, G. D., H. R. Wyatt, J. O. Hill, B. G. McGuckin, C. Brill, B. S. Mohammed, et al. 2003. A randomized trial of a low-carbohydrate diet for obesity. *New England Journal of Medicine* 348:2082-2090.

Gluck, M. E., A. Geliebter, and T. Satov. 2001. Night eating syndrome is associated with depression, low self-esteem, reduced daytime hunger, and less weight loss in obese outpatients. *Obesity Research* 9:264-267.

Goran, M. F., G. D. Ball, and M. L. Cruz. 2003. Obesity and risk of type 2 diabetes and cardiovascular disease in children and adults. *Journal of Clinical Endocrinology and Metabolism* 88: 1417-1427.

Gupta, M. A. 1991. Sleep-related eating in bulimia nervosa—an underreported parasomnia disorder. *Sleep Research* 20:182.

Hajak, G., A. Rodenbeck, J. Staedt, B. Bandelow, G. Huether, and E. Ruther. 1995. Nocturnal plasma melatonin levels in patients suffering from chronic primary insomnia. *Journal of Pineal Research* 19:116-122.

Hsu, L. K. G., S. Betancourt, and S. P. Sullivan. 1996. Eating disturbances before and after vertical banded gastroplasty: A pilot study. *International Journal of Eating Disorders* 19:23-34. Introduction.

Kennedy, S. H., P. E. Garinkel, V. Parienti, D. Costa, and G. M. Brown. 1989. Changes in melatonin levels but not cortisol levels are associated with depression in patients with eating disorders. *Archives in General Psychiatry* 46:73-78.

Kessler, R. C., K. A. McGonagle, S. Zhao, C. B. Nelson, M. Hughes, S. Eshleman, et al. 1994. Lifetime and 12-month prevalence of DSM-II-R psychiatric disorders in the United States: Results from the National Comorbidity Survey. *Archives of General Psychiatry* 52:374-383.

Kuratsune, H., K. Yamaguti, M. Sawada, S. Kodate, T. Machii, Y. Kanakura, et al. 1998. Dehydroepiandrosterone sulfate deficiency in chronic fatigue syndrome. *International Journal of Molecular Medicine* 1:143-146.

Ljung, T., G. Holm, P. Friberg, B. Andersson, B. A. Bengtsson, J. Svensson, et al. 2000. The activity of the hypothalamic-pituitary-adrenal axis and the sympathetic nervous system in relation to waist/hip circumference ratio in men. *Obesity Research* 8:487-495.

Mokdad, A. H., B. A. Bowman, E. S. Ford, F. Vinicor, J. S. Marks, and J. P. Koplan. 2001. The continuing epidemics of obesity and diabetes in the United States. *Journal of the American Medical Association* 286:1195-1200.

Morin, C. M. 2001. Combined treatments of insomnia. In *Combined Treatments for Mental Disorders: A Guide to Psychological and Pharmacological Interventions,* edited by M. T. Sammons and N. B. Schmidt. Washington, D.C.: American Psychological Association.

Morton, R. 1694. *Phthisiologia (A Treatise of Consumptions)*. London: Printed for Sam Smith and Benj. Walford.

Napolitano, M. A., S. Head, M. A. Babyak, and J. A. Blumenthal. 2001. Binge eating disorder and night eating syndrome: Psychological and behavioral characteristics. *International Journal of Eating Disorders* 30:193-203.

O'Reardon, J. P., B. Ringel, D. F. Dinges, K. C. Allison, N. L. Rogers, N. S. Martino, et al. 2004. Circadian eating and sleeping patterns in the night eating syndrome. Working paper, University of Pennsylvania, School of Medicine, Department of Psychiatry at Philadelphia.

O'Reardon, J. P., A. J. Stunkard, and K. C. Allison. In press. A clinical trial of sertraline in the treatment of the night eating syndrome. *International Journal of Eating Disorders*.

Pawlow, L. A., P. M. O'Neil, and R. J. Malcolm. 2003. Night eating syndrome: Effects of brief relaxation training on stress, mood, hunger, and eating patterns. *International Journal of Obesity and Related Metabolic Disorders* 27(8):970-978.

Powers, P. S., A. Perez, F. Boyd, and A. Rosemurgy. 1999. Eating pathology before and after bariatric surgery: A prospective study. *International Journal of Eating Disorders* 25:293-300.

Raber J. 1998. Detrimental effects of chronic hypothalamic-pituitary-adrenal axis activation. From obesity to memory deficits. *Molecular Neurobiology* 18:1-22.

Rand, C. S. W., M. D. Macgregor, and A. J. Stunkard. 1997. The night eating syndrome in the general population and among postoperative obesity surgery patients. *International Journal of Eating Disorders* 22:65-69.

Schenck, C. H., and M. W. Mahowald. 1994. Review of nocturnal sleep-related eating disorders. *International Journal of Eating Disorders* 15:343-356.

Schiffman, S. S., and C. A. Gatlin. 1993. Sweeteners: State of knowledge review. *Neuroscience and Biobehavioral Reviews* 17:313-345.

Schlundt, D. G., J. O. Hill, T. Sbrocco, J. Pope-Cordle, and T. Sharp. 1992. The role of breakfast in the treatment of obesity: A randomized clinical trial. *American Journal of Nutrition* 55:645-651.

Sinha, R., G. Fisch, B. Teague, W. V. Tamborlane, B. Banyas, K. Allen, et al. 2002. Prevalence of impaired glucose tolerance among children and adolescents with marked obesity. *New England Journal of Medicine* 346:801-810.

Stunkard, A. J. 1959. Eating patterns and obesity. *Psychiatric Quarterly* 33:284-294.

Stunkard, A. J., R. Berkowitz, T. Wadden, C. Tanrikut, E. Reiss, and L. Young. 1996. Binge eating disorder and night-eating syndrome. *International Journal of Obesity and Related Metabolic Disorders* 20:1-6.

Stunkard, A. J., W. J. Grace, and H. G. Wolff. 1955. The night-eating syndrome: A pattern of food intake among certain obese patients. *American Journal of Medicine* 19:78-86.

Stunkard, A. J., J. R. Harris, N. L. Pedersen, and G. E. McClearn. 1990. The body mass index of twins who have been reared apart. *New England Journal of Medicine* 322:1483-1487.

Szabo, A., E. Billett, and J. Turner. 2001. Phenylethylamine, a possible link to the antidepressant effects of exercise? *British Journal of Sports Medicine* 35(5):342-343.

Williamson, D. A., O. D. Lawson, S. M. Bennett, and L. Hinz. 1989. Behavioral treatment of night bingeing and rumination in an adult case of bulimia nervosa. *Journal of Behavior Therapy & Experimental Psychiatry* 20:73-77.

Kelly C. Allison, Ph.D., is an instructor at the University of Pennsylvania School of Medicine. She received her BA from the University of Notre Dame in 1995 and her MA and Ph.D. from Miami University in 1997 and 2000, respectively. Her research interests include characterizing and treating night eating syndrome. She is also interested in the effects of sociocultural influences on eating disordered attitudes and behavior.

Albert Stunkard, MD, is professor of psychiatry at the University of Pennsylvania School of Medicine, where he founded the Weight and Eating Disorders Program, of which he is currently director emeritus. He received a BS from Yale University in 1943 and an MD from Columbia University in 1945. He is the author of nearly 400 publications, mostly in the field of obesity, and his research has been supported for forty years by the National Institutes of Health.

Sara L. Thier currently works in the Quality of Care Program Area of the Robert Wood Johnson Foundation in Princeton, NJ. She received her BA from the University of Michigan, Ann Arbor in 1987, her MPH at UCLA in 1991, and is currently working on her Ph.D. in health policy.

Some Other
New Harbinger Titles

The End of-life Handbook, Item 5112 $15.95

The Mindfulness and Acceptance Workbook for Anxiety, Item 4993 $21.95

A Cancer Patient's Guide to Overcoming Depression and Anxiety, Item 5044 $19.95

Handbook of Clinical Psychopharmacology for Therapists, 5th edition, Item 5358 $55.95

Disarming the Narcissist, Item 5198 $14.95

The ABCs of Human Behavior, Item 5389 $49.95

Rage, Item 4627 $14.95

10 Simple Solutions to Chronic Pain, Item 4825 $12.95

The Estrogen-Depression Connection, Item 4832 $16.95

Helping Your Socially Vulnerable Child, Item 4580 $15.95

Life Planning for Adults with Developmental Disabilities, Item 4511 $19.95

Overcoming Fear of Heights, Item 4566 $14.95

Acceptance & Commitment Therapy for the Treatment of Post-Traumatic Stress Disorder & Trauma-Related Problems, Item 4726 $58.95

But I Didn't Mean That!, Item 4887 $14.95

Calming Your Anxious Mind, 2nd edition, Item 4870 $14.95

10 Simple Solutions for Building Self-Esteem, Item 4955 $12.95

The Dialectical Behavior Therapy Skills Workbook, Item 5136 $21.95

The Family Intervention Guide to Mental Illness, Item 5068 $17.95

Finding Life Beyond Trauma, Item 4979 $19.95

Five Good Minutes at Work, Item 4900 $14.95

It's So Hard to Love You, Item 4962 $14.95

Energy Tapping for Trauma, Item 5013 $17.95

Thoughts & Feelings, 3rd edition, Item 5105 $19.95

Transforming Depression, Item 4917 $12.95

Helping A Child with Nonverbal Learning Disorder, 2nd edition, Item 5266 $15.95

Leave Your Mind Behind, Item 5341 $14.95

Learning ACT, Item 4986 $44.95

ACT for Depression, Item 5099 $42.95

Integrative Treatment for Adult ADHD, Item 5211 $49.95

Freeing the Angry Mind, Item 4380 $14.95

Call **toll free, 1-800-748-6273,** or log on to our online bookstore a **www.newharbinger.com** to order. Have your Visa or Mastercard number ready. C send a check for the titles you want to New Harbinger Publications, Inc., 5674 Shattuc Ave., Oakland, CA 94609. Include $4.50 for the first book and 75¢ for each addition book, to cover shipping and handling. (California residents please include appropria sales tax.) Allow two to five weeks for delivery.

Prices subject to change without notice.